A Guide to the New Testament

ALICE PARMELEE

These things are written that you may believe
that Jesus is the Christ, the Son of God, and
that believing you may have life in his name.

John 20:31

MOREHOUSE-BARLOW CO.
Wilton, Connecticut

The cover illustration is used by permission of the Cathedral Church of Saints Peter and Paul, Washington, D.C.

The Scripture quotations in this book, unless attributed otherwise, are from the Revised Standard Version of the Bible, copyrighted 1946, 1952, ©1971, 1973 by the Division of Christian Education of the National Council of the Churches of Christ in the U.S.A., and used by permission.

Copyright ©1980 Alice Parmelee
All rights reserved

Morehouse-Barlow Co., Inc.
78 Danbury Road, Wilton, Connecticut 06897

ISBN-0-8192-1255-5

Library of Congress Catalog Card Number 79-87 617

Printed in the United States of America

Contents

Preface 5
Abbreviations 7
How to Look up Bible References 9
The New Testament

    Introduction 11
    Matthew 16
    Mark 22
    Luke 28
    John 35
    Acts 41
    Romans 48
    1 Corinthians 52
    2 Corinthians 56
    Galatians 60
    Ephesians 63
    Philippians 66
    Colossians 70
    1 Thessalonians 73
    2 Thessalonians 76
    1 Timothy 79
    2 Timothy 82
    Titus 84
    Philemon 85

Hebrews	87
James	91
1 Peter	93
2 Peter	96
1 John	99
2 John	101
3 John	102
Jude	103
Revelation	105

The Deeds and Words of Jesus Christ 112
 —a Harmony of the Gospels

The Parables of Jesus 122

The Miracles of Jesus 129

The Prayers of Jesus and His Followers 133

An Outline of the Life of Paul 138

Selected Bibliography 141

Index 143

Preface

This third volume of the *All About the Bible* series attempts to provide readers, students, and teachers with the sort of knowledge that makes informed reading of the New Testament possible. Most of us are acquainted with its chief stories and know its incandescent verses by heart, but we often experience difficulty in reading its twenty-seven documents. These "title-deeds of the Christian faith," written two thousands years ago as continuing testimony to the fact of Christ, make great demands upon our understanding. The modern reader, however, has many sources of help, including the traditions and teachings of the Church, five or six excellent and readable English translations, and a vast and varied body of literature that explains and interprets almost all aspects of these basic Christian documents. From numerous sources I have tried to select the most helpful materials and to present them as clearly and concisely as possible. With increased knowledge of the background of the New Testament and some understanding of the viewpoints and personal experiences of its authors, readers of these ancient books are better equipped to discover for themselves the meaning of Christ and his living message for today.

The major part of this volume examines the New Testament book by book, sketching the background and contents of each one and calling attention to some of its most valuable insights.

Next, a table outlining the deeds and words of Jesus as reported in the Gospels, is arranged in four parallel columns, so that readers can see where the respective texts agree, or where one Gospel contains material not included in the others. This simplified harmony or synopsis also serves as a table of contents of the Gospels themselves.

To provide a basis for detailed study of important aspects of the New Testament and to help readers live themselves into the Gospels, there are three short chapters dealing with the parables, the miracles, and the prayers of Jesus. These three forms often convey to us his actual voice and the true meaning of his "good news." Included with the prayers of Jesus are those of his followers.

Finally, a brief outline of the life of the apostle Paul establishes a foundation for further study of this towering figure and brings this volume to a close.

Because this book, like the others in this series, is based upon the wisdom and insight of many, especially the 20th-century scholars of the New Testament, I owe them all a debt of gratitude. I particularly want to thank: Pierson Parker, former professor of the literature and interpretation of the New Testament at General Theological Seminary, New York, for his advice, graciously given; Margaret Sheriff, for her continuing support; and my sister Mary, for help with all aspects of this book.

Alice Parmelee

Abbreviations

ABBREVIATIONS

For the Books of the Bible

Old Testament

Genesis	Gen	Ecclesiastes	Eccles
Exodus	Ex	Song of Solomon	Song
Leviticus	Lev	Isaiah	Isa
Numbers	Num	Jeremiah	Jer
Deuteronomy	Deut	Lamentations	Lam
Joshua	Josh	Ezekiel	Ezek
Judges	Judg	Daniel	Dan
Ruth	Ruth	Hosea	Hos
1 Samuel	1 Sam	Joel	Joel
2 Samuel	2 Sam	Amos	Amos
1 Kings	1 Kings	Obadiah	Obad
2 Kings	2 Kings	Jonah	Jonah
1 Chronicles	1 Chron	Micah	Mic
2 Chronicles	2 Chron	Nahum	Nahum
Ezra	Ezra	Habakkuk	Hab
Nehemiah	Neh	Zephaniah	Zeph
Esther	Esther	Haggai	Hag
Job	Job	Zechariah	Zech
Psalms	Ps	Malachi	Mal
Proverbs	Prov		

New Testament

Matthew	Mt	1 Timothy	1 Tim
Mark	Mk	2 Timothy	2 Tim
Luke	Lk	Titus	Titus
John	Jn	Philemon	Philem
Acts of the Apostles	Acts	Hebrews	Heb
Romans	Rom	James	Jas
1 Corinthians	1 Cor	1 Peter	1 Pet
2 Corinthians	2 Cor	2 Peter	2 Pet
Galatians	Gal	1 John	1 Jn
Ephesians	Eph	2 John	2 Jn
Philippians	Phil	3 John	3 Jn
Colossians	Col	Jude	Jude
1 Thessalonians	1 Thess	Revelation	Rev
2 Thessalonians	2 Thess		

Other Abbreviations

A.D.	*Anno Domini*—"in the year of our Lord"
B.C.	Before Christ
c.	*circa*—"about," used with uncertain dates
KJV	King James Version (Authorized Version)
NEB	New English Bible
N.T.	New Testament
O.T.	Old Testament
RSV	Revised Standard Version
v., vv.	Verse, verses

How to Look up Bible References

Jn 3:16—means the Gospel according to John, chapter 3, verse 16

Mic 6:5,8—means the Book of Micah, chapter 6, verse 5 and verse 8

2 Cor 5:17-19—means the Second Letter to the Corinthians, chapter 5, verse 17 to 19 inclusive

Jer 8:7; 9:3—means Jeremiah, chapter 8, verse 7; and also chapter 9, verse 3

Mt 5:2-7:28—means the Gospel according to Matthew, chapter 5, verse 2, to chapter 7, verse 28 inclusive

Mt 5-7—means Matthew, chapter 5 through chapter 7

Mk 8:29; Lk 9:20—means Mark, chapter 8, verse 29; and Luke, chapter 9, verse 20

Horace Knowles — British & Foreign Bible Society, London

THE NEW TESTAMENT

Introduction

Basically, the New Testament is the story of something that occurred in the eastern Mediterranean world during the early decades of the Roman Empire to change the outlook of human life and alter the course of history. This occurrence, of which the New Testament is the chief documentary evidence, lit up the human sky with a hope that has never been extinguished. Indeed, the New Testament is primarily a book of good news and of hope. Its chief event is recognized in the calendar of the western world by the division of history into two eras: B.C. (before Christ) and A.D. (*anno domini*—"in the year of our Lord").

The twenty-seven books of the New Testament, varied though they are in point of view and literary form, speak with a single voice of one underlying reality. They believe that Jesus Christ, who "reflects the glory of God and bears the very stamp of his nature" (Heb 1:3), bridged the abyss that separates man from God and brought healing and new life to the human family. Into a world rife with despair came the angel's song of the "good news of a great joy." The good news caught on like wildfire. Jesus proclaimed the kingdom of God and crowds flocked to listen to his message and witness his wonderful works that signified the power of God active in their midst. Now and again, perhaps, someone recorded in writing something that Jesus had said or done, but the main effort of the earliest years was to spread the good news by word of mouth as widely as possible before the expected, imminent arrival of God's kingdom. Thus it was that at least thirty-five years elapsed after the resurrection before Mark sat down to write his brief, straightforward account.

"Here begins," he wrote, "the Gospel of Jesus Christ the Son of God" (Mk 1:1, NEB). Because he recorded his story in Greek, his actual word was the Greek *euangelion*, "good news," which was later translated into Anglo-Saxon as *godspell*, "glad tidings." From this word, *gospel* is derived. Jesus himself had called his proclamation of the kingdom the "good news" (Lk 4:18; Mk 1:14-15). In the letters of Paul, *gospel* means the good news of the Lord Jesus Christ illuminated in the light of the resurrection. This was the apostolic message (Rom 1:1-6,16). Mark, writing soon after the martyrdoms of two of the foremost apostles, Peter and Paul, offered the same apostolic message of faith—the same gospel—but in a written form.

Gospel, the distinctive title of Mark's testimony to the new faith, was subsequently applied to similar works by Matthew and Luke and also to John's somewhat different book. Matthew's Gospel is longer and more elaborate than Mark's, for the author's purpose was possibly to revise and "improve" Mark by adding large blocks of new material, chiefly comprising the teachings of Jesus. The third Gospel, that by Luke, is thought to be based on Mark and on some of the same sources used by Matthew. Luke's Gospel is really the first volume of a two-volume history outlining the beginnings of Christianity. His second volume is, of course, the Acts of the Apostles. John's Gospel tells fundamentally the same story as that of the earlier three, though its distinctive style and depth of interpretation make it unique.

All of the Gospels were written by men of faith to strengthen the faith of others and to spread the good news. Although these books were not intended to be biographies of Jesus and lack much of the information we would like to have, they do portray him vividly, consistently, and with remarkable agreement. At a time when fanciful tales were beginning to be fabricated and strange doctrines proposed, the Gospels aimed to establish a reliable record of what Jesus had said and done. They were written to preserve the memory of the unique revelation of God in the midst of human history—a revelation witnessed and proclaimed by the apostles and believed and taught by the Church. Finally, in the words of John, the Gospels were "written that you may believe that Jesus is the Christ, the Son of God, and that believing you may have life in his name" (Jn 20:31).

In Acts and the twenty-one Epistles or Letters that follow, the impact of the Christian good news on a disillusioned and largely pagan world is sketched dramatically. The apostle Paul dominates three-quarters of Acts and is believed to be the author of nine or ten of the chief Letters that define what Christianity really is. Because he wrote to particular churches or individuals in response to definite situations, his communications accord with the definition of a letter. Later, however, these letters were published and read by the Church at large, thus taking on the character of formal essays or treatises concerning Christian life and doctrine. As such they can be viewed as epistles and are so named in the King James Version.

The three Pastoral Epistles (from the Latin *pastor* "shepherd") include 1 and 2 Timothy and Titus. They advise young ministers how to preserve and defend their own faith and that of their spiritual flocks.

Hebrews, a carefully argued, theological discussion, contains a moving chapter on faith and one of the great interpretations of the person and mission of Jesus Christ. Following it are seven miscellaneous letters. These are sometimes called the "Catholic" Epistles (from the Greek *katholicos* "general," "universal") because, with the exception of 2 and 3 John, they are addressed to churches in general rather than to particular churches. James may be a sermon on Christian living; 1 Peter is a ringing call to courage and hope; 2 Peter is the latest book of the New Testament to be written; 1 John deals with the essentials of Christianity; 2 John is a message to a local church; 3 John is a private note; and Jude is a letter against heresy.

The New Testament ends in the stirring finale of Revelation, a strange, overwhelming message that was born in a crisis of suffering and despair, but has continued to nourish Christian hope with its promise of ultimate victory. Such are the books of the New Testament in which we read the message of God's gifts of hope, deliverance, and abundant life through faith in Jesus Christ.

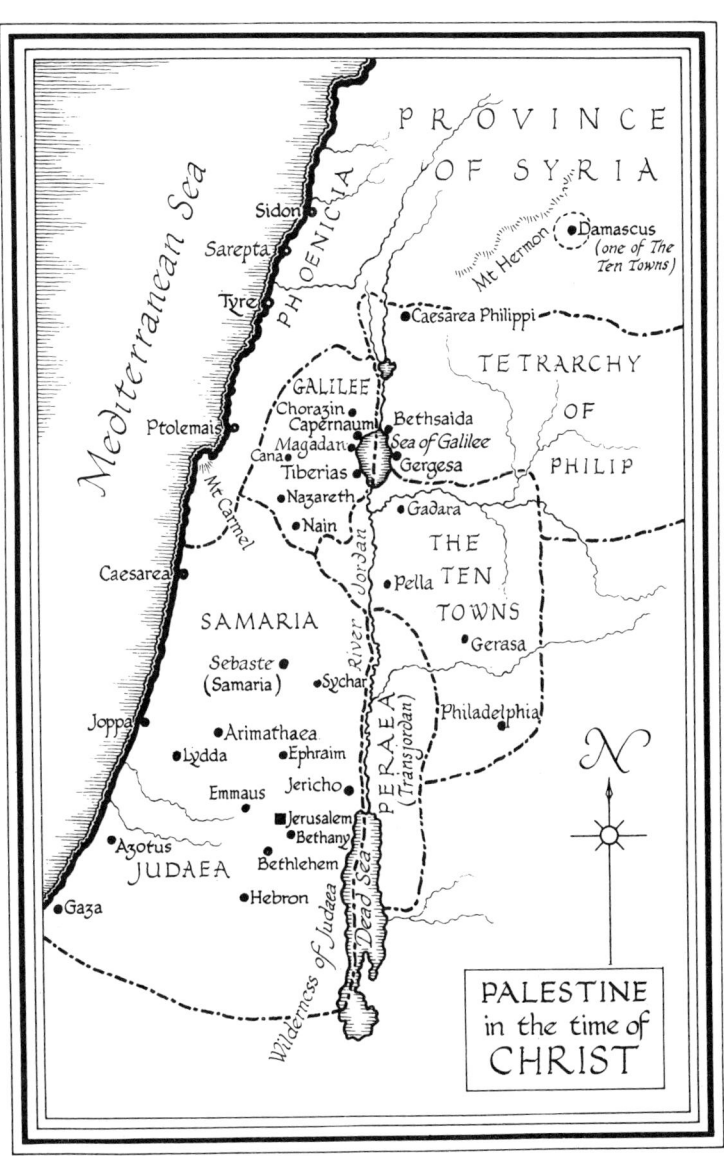

Horace Knowles — British & Foreign Bible Society, London

The Gospel According to Matthew

A Comprehensive Record of the Words and Deeds of Jesus Christ

Position: First Gospel, 1st book of the New Testament

Date: Between A.D. 75 and 85

Sources: Possibly the Gospel of Mark; the hypothetical source, Q; a collection of Old Testament prophecies relating to Christ; special material used only by Matthew

Author: An unknown Christian, probably of Jewish background

Style: Powerful, direct, clear, great economy of words in the sayings of Jesus

Written for: Jewish Christians, possibly of Antioch in Syria

Purpose: To provide an authoritative handbook of the Christian faith

Themes: Jesus is the Messiah of Old Testament prophecy; his Church is the New Israel and the people of God's New Covenant; his teachings comprise God's new Law

Contents:

1. The coming of Jesus Christ, the Messiah (1:1-4:11)
   a. His genealogy, birth, and infancy (1-2)
   b. His baptism and temptation (3:1-4:11)
2. Jesus in Galilee (4:12-16:28)
   a. The beginning of his ministry (4:12-25)
   b. First discourse—the Sermon on the Mount (5-7)

c. Narratives of his healing and teaching (8-9)
   d. Second discourse—instruction of the twelve disciples (10)
   e. Growing opposition (11-12)
   f. Third discourse—parables of the kingdom (13)
3. Jesus in exile: miracles, healings, teachings (14-16)
4. His Messiahship (17-20)
   a. The transfiguration (17)
   b. Fourth discourse—on true discipleship (18)
   c. Events and teachings on the way to Jerusalem (19-20)
5. His final week in Jerusalem (21:1-26:16)
   a. His challenge (21-22)
   b. Denunciation of the scribes and Pharisees (23)
   c. Fifth discourse—on the end of the age (24-25)
   d. The conspiracy; his anointing; the treachery of Judas (26:1-16)
6. Last supper, arrest, trials, crucifixion, burial (26:17-27:66)
7. The resurrection; his commission to his apostles (28)

Introduction:

When the four Gospels were issued as a collection, Matthew was accorded the first place, despite the fact that Mark was probably the older work. Later, Christians must have regarded the First Gospel as a revised and improved edition of Mark and therefore the fullest and most authoritative record of the life and teachings of Jesus. Moreover, church leaders found its contents well arranged for teaching purposes. Matthew reproduced nine-tenths of Mark's text but inserted into Mark's biographical framework five blocks of other material. Each of these five blocks, which are labeled "discourse" in the outline above, ends with the formula, "when Jesus finished these sayings." The five discourses are actually collections of Jesus' teachings grouped according to subject. In number they are, of course, similar to the five Old Testament books of the Law, a fact suggesting that the moral teaching of Jesus is closely connected to the Law. "Think not that I have come to abolish the law and the prophets; I have come not to abolish them but to fulfil them" (5:17).

The source from which Matthew derived many of the sayings of Jesus appears to have been used by Luke also because these two Gospels contain more than two hundred verses in common, none of which is found in Mark. This shared source is believed to have been a document that contained an anthology of Jesus' words. It is designated as Q, from the German *Quelle*, "source." Was Q the *Logia* referred to by Bishop Papias when he wrote, c. A.D. 130, "Matthew collected the *Logia* in the Hebrew language and each one interpreted them as he was able"? If the apostle Matthew actually recorded the sayings of Jesus, it is easy to understand why the Gospel in which they are an important feature was named for him.

The distinct style in which the sayings and teachings of Jesus are phrased in the New Testament reveals an original mind that was swift and direct, poetic and imaginative, a mind that expressed itself with unmistakable authority. The Biblical scholar, Charles H. Dodd, in *The Founder of Christianity*, observes that the teachings of Jesus are "in the form of short, crisp utterances, pungent, often allusive, even cryptic, laden with irony and paradox . . . he speaks in concrete images and pictures in preference to general or abstract propositions." The discourses in Matthew, the memorable sayings preserved in Mark, and the stories and sayings in Luke, despite the fact that they were preserved in the memories of the apostles and other early Christians and later translated from their original Aramaic, the language spoken by Jesus, into Greek and eventually into English, nevertheless give an impression of a unique and living personality and bring us vividly into the presence of Jesus himself.

Besides Mark and Q, this Gospel possibly used a collection of Old Testament prophecies concerning the Messiah that are believed to have been translated into Greek prior to the writing of Matthew. (According to one theory, this collection, rather than Q, comprised the *Logia* referred to by Papias.)

Other materials in Matthew that cannot be traced to Mark, Q, or the Old Testament prophecies include: events connected with Jesus' birth, Peter's walking on the water, the Temple tax found in the fish's mouth, the fate of Judas, the dream of Pilate's wife, Pilate's washing of his hands, the earthquake and the strange happenings at the death of Jesus, the sealing of the tomb, and the appearances of the risen Christ to the women and the disciples. The legendary quality of some of these stories suggests that they may have been traditions handed down orally for many years by the Aramaic-speaking Christians of Jerusalem.

The special viewpoints of this Gospel arise from the fact that its author was probably a Jewish Christian writing, not for Gentiles, but for Christians who, like himself, had been nurtured in Judaism. To these readers he demonstrated that Jesus of Nazareth is the Messiah whose coming was foretold by the Old Testament prophets. He showed how Christ fulfills God's promises to his people and how the new Law of Christ supplants and completes the old Law of Moses. Throughout the book messianic prophecies are linked with events in the life of Jesus and are often accompanied by the phrase, "that the scriptures might be fulfilled."

Matthew dealt also with death and judgment, concerns

Christ Healing the Sick -- Rembrandt (c. 1649)

The Pierpont Morgan Library

In this etching Rembrandt translates Matthew 19:1-22 into visual images that portray the sick, the Pharisees, the rich young man, Peter, the parents, the children, and a chance onlooker, each one responding in his or her own way to Christ.

that had engaged Jewish thought for two centuries. He introduced the characteristic words and ideas of an apocalypse into some of the sayings of Jesus (8:12; 13:42; 22:13; etc.) and included a long apocalyptic discourse (24-25).

This is the only Gospel that refers directly to the Church (16:18; 18:17). The author's particular interest in the Church and its everyday problems is shown by his inclusion of the teachings of Jesus on such matters as: almsgiving, prayer, fasting (6:1-18), marriage and divorce (5:27-32; 19:3-12), faithfulness under persecution (10:17-36; 16:24-28), treatment of an offending brother (18:15-22).

Matthew, who as a Jew believed that the Jewish people existed for the sake of their God and his worship, beheld a wider vision when he became a Christian, and wrote of a universal Church open to all, both Jews and Gentiles. Though this Gospel begins with Jesus' descent from Abraham and David, it ends in a catholic spirit by proclaiming both the worldwide kingdom of God and the eternally present Christ (28:19-20).

* * * *

In an emergency today, private motor vehicles can be commandeered by the police, just as a first-century Roman soldier in the Palestinian army of occupation could order a citizen to carry his pack for one mile. Jesus, commenting on this military requirement, which was extremely offensive to Jewish pride, urged generous cooperation (Mt 5:41).

* * * *

Scriptural justification for the anti-Semitism that stains the pages of history has been based on the fanatical shout of the adherents of the Sanhedrin at the trial of Jesus, "His blood be on us and on our children" (Mt 27:25). Only Matthew's Gospel records these reckless words of the crowd, which the other Gospels identify, not as the common people of Jerusalem, but as those whom "the chief priests stirred up" (Mk 15:11).

* * * *

Surely there must be a place for righteous indignation, mused an ancient Biblical copyist as he set down the warning of Jesus that "every one who is angry with his brother shall be liable to judgment" (Mt 5:22). Accordingly, he undertook to "improve" the statement by inserting, after the word *brother*, the escape clause "without cause" or "thoughtlessly."

* * * *

Sea birds that seem to walk or paddle on the surface of the water are called "little Peters" or petrels in honor of the disciple who tried to walk on the Sea of Galilee (Mt 14:29).

The Gospel According to Mark

The Earliest Gospel

Position: Second Gospel, 2nd book of the New Testament

Date: Between A.D. 65 and 75

Sources: The oral tradition of the early Church concerning the mission, message, and death of Jesus; possible records of Peter's sermons; other vanished documents

Author: Conceivably, John Mark, cousin of Barnabas and companion of Paul and Peter

Style: Unpolished, vivid, terse, dramatic, colorful, filled with specific details, conversational in tone

The Gospel According to Mark 23

Written for: Greek-speaking, Gentile Christians probably of Rome

Purposes: To show, by his words and deeds, what Jesus was like; to instill courage in a Church facing martyrdom; to provide an authoritative record for Church use

Theme: The faith that Jesus of Nazareth is the Christ, the Son of God

Contents:
1. Introduction—Jesus and John the Baptist (1:1-13)
2. Jesus' ministry in Galilee and elsewhere (1:14-8:26)
   a. Near the Sea of Galilee (1:14-5:43)
   b. More distant journeys (6:1-8:26)
3. The Messiah and his coming death (8:27-9:50)
   a. Peter's confession (8:27-30)
   b. Predictions of the passion (8:31-33; 9:30-32)
   c. The cost of discipleship (8:34-9:1, 33-37; 10:13- 31, 35-45)
   d. The transfiguration and the healing of the epileptic boy (9:2-29)
   e. Various sayings (9:38-50)
4. Events during Jesus' journey to Jerusalem (10)
5. Jesus in Jerusalem (11-13)
   a. His triumphal entry (11:1-11)
   b. His ministry in the city (11:12-12:44)
   c. Apocalyptic discourse (13)
6. The narrative of Jesus' death (14-15)
7. The three women at the empty tomb (16:1-8)
8. The longer ending to Mark (16:9-20)

Introduction:

This oldest of the Gospels is the shortest, but historically it is the most important because it is believed to be the earliest surviving written record of the words and deeds of Jesus and it may have formed the basis for the Gospels of Matthew and Luke. By studying the relation of these later Gospels to the Gospel of Mark, it becomes evident that these two are really expanded editions of Mark. The Gospel of John is also dependent upon Mark, but to a lesser extent. Thus Mark is the prime historical source for the facts undergirding Christianity. Not long after it appeared, the more expertly written Gospels of Matthew and Luke supplanted it in popular favor, but Mark, though neglected, was not discarded, as were other early documentary sources. Its survival may have been due to the circumstance that it was a treasured document of the influential Roman church for which it was probably written.

The tradition that John Mark wrote this Gospel in Rome soon after the death of Peter is supported by documentary evidence from the 1st and 2nd centuries. The First Letter of Peter, which might have been written in the apostle's name near the end of the 1st century, closes with a statement indicating that Mark was with Peter in Rome. "She who is at Babylon [a cryptic name suggesting Rome] . . . sends you greetings; and so does my son Mark" (1 Pet 5:13). This was the John Mark whose mother's large house in Jerusalem became a meeting place for the early Christians (Acts 12:12-17). Mark joined his cousin Barnabas in Antioch and from there set sail with him and Paul on their first missionary journey (Acts 12:25; 13:5). Despite Paul's early lack of confidence in Mark, the two men were eventually reunited in missionary work (Col 4:10; 2 Tim 4:11).

Mark's association with Peter, and his probable use of material from Peter's sermons as one of the sources of his Gospel is documented in a statement made by Papias, bishop of Hieropolis c. A.D. 130, but based on earlier evidence from a church official known as the Elder John. According to Papias' statement (preserved in Eusebius' 4th-century *Church History*),

> The Elder used to say the following: Mark, who became the interpreter of Peter, wrote accurately as much as he remembered of the Lord's sayings or doings, but he did not write these in their order. For he had not himself heard the Lord nor been his personal follower, but was later, as I said, a follower of Peter, who used to adapt his teaching to the occasion, but not as though he were framing an ordered account of the Lord's sayings. So Mark made no error when he wrote some things as he remembered them. For he had only one purpose—to leave out nothing and to falsify none of the things he had heard.

The probable date and place of origin of the Second Gospel are suggested in the fragmentary document now called the *Anti-Marcionite Prologue to Mark*, c. A.D. 160-180, which states, "Mark . . . who is called 'Stumpfingered' because he had small fingers in comparison to the size of his body . . . was Peter's interpreter. After the death of Peter, he wrote this Gospel in the regions of Italy."

The historical value of Mark is attested in the fragment from Papias who emphasized the book's apostolic authority, its accuracy, completeness, and freedom from false statements. Mark was clearly not a neutral historian, but a deeply-committed member of the early Church who recorded conscientiously the testimony of the first Christians in the light of the Church's faith. The main sequence of events in his Gospel is believed to preserve, in broad outline, the course of Jesus' ministry.

An outstanding characteristic of this Gospel is its headlong pace accentuated by no less than forty repetitions of the word *immediately*, by many condensed episodes, and by sentences strung together with "and . . . and." Vivid eyewitness details convey the tone of the Church's early oral teaching and seem to echo Peter's words (1:20, 33, 41, 43; 3:34; 4:38; 10:22; etc.). From the oral period of Christian tradition come this Gospel's so-called pronouncement stories, which were shaped in such a way that each one preserves a single memorable saying of Jesus (2:18-20; 10:2-9, 13-16; 12:13-17; etc.). Mark explains Jewish customs 7:3-4; 15:42; etc.) and translates Aramaic expressions (5:41; 7:11, 34; 15:22; etc.)—an indication that this Gospel was written for non-Jewish, Greek-speaking readers.

The entire Gospel concentrates upon Jesus. In writing for Gentile Christians, Mark attempted to answer the question they must have asked him frequently, "What was Jesus really like?" Mark showed him in the fullness of his humanity as a man among his fellow-countrymen, eating and drinking (2:16; 14:3), becoming weary and sleeping (4:38), touching those who asked for healing (5:41; 6:5), and expressing a broad range of human emotions (3:5; 5:19; 6:6; 10:14,21; 14:33, 15:34). These vivid notes of his genuine humanity and of his common sense produce an unforgettable portrait. Mark also portrayed Jesus in his divine power proclaiming the kingdom of God, forgiving sins, expelling demons, healing the sick, and speaking words incandescent in their authority and truth. Mark thus produced a wealth of evidence to support the basic belief of the Church and the thesis of his own Gospel that "Jesus Christ [is] the Son of God" (1:1).

The Gospel begins with a shout in the wilderness, the proclamation of the coming of the Mighty One. Despite the shadow of the cross that falls upon Jesus' ministry from its beginning (2:6-7; 3:6), the narrative continues at a rapid pace to its first turning point in Peter's declaration, "You are the Christ" (8:29). It goes on to a second turning when the high priest questions Jesus at his trial, "Are you the Christ, the Son of the Blessed?" and Jesus replies, "I am" (14:61-62). The Gospel reaches its climax at Jesus' death when he utters his cry of victory. A pagan centurion, certain at last of who Jesus is, declares that a divine being has died (15:39). The book closes with the discovery of the empty tomb and the angel's statement, "He is risen" (16:6).

This well-constructed Gospel, which triumphantly records the resurrection, breaks off abruptly on an unexpected note of fear and silence: "they said nothing to any one, for they were afraid." This unlikely end for an otherwise powerful and carefully planned document raises questions for which there are no conclusive answers. Was the Gospel unfinished or did its original ending become lost at an early date? In the first century, someone who wrote in a style different from that of Mark prepared a summary of Christ's resurrection appearances for the end of the Gospel (16:9-20).

* * * *

In medieval legends the cup that Jesus blessed at the last supper and gave to his disciples (Mk 14:23) was called the Holy Grail. According to the apocryphal *Gospel of Nicodemus*, Joseph of Arimathea took the cup from the table after the supper. His relatives later carried it to England where many miracles were attributed to it before it was finally lost. The Arthurian legends narrate the quest for the Holy Grail by Galahad (or Parsifal, in other traditions). When a silver goblet decorated with Christian symbols was unearthed at Antioch in 1910, it was thought to date from the first century and some people believed that it had been made to enclose the Holy Grail. Further study has proved that this so-called Chalice of Antioch, now in the Cloisters of the Metropolitan Museum of Art, New York, is a 4th-century Christian chalice.

* * * *

Among the intriguing details in this Gospel is that of the young man who "ran away naked" from those who arrested Jesus (Mk 14:51-52). Who was he? Why was he there? Why is he mentioned at all? It has been suggested that he was Mark himself who here recorded his only connection with the gospel story as a sort of "artist's signature in the corner of his painting." It is possible, however, that the incident was inspired by Amos 2:16.

The Gospel According to Luke

The Gospel of the Lovingkindness of Jesus

Position:	Third Gospel, 3rd book of the New Testament
Date:	Between A.D. 75 and 85
Sources:	Perhaps the Gospel of Mark, Q, and special material from oral and written sources
Author:	Possibly Luke, Paul's Gentile companion who is described as "the beloved physician" (Col 4:14)

The Gospel According to Luke

Style: Polished, sensitive, graceful

Written for: Gentile Christians perhaps of Antioch or Rome

Purpose: To compile from existing records an account of "all that Jesus began to do and teach" (Acts 1:1) so that Gentile Christians might have an accurate, well-planned, authoritative, and easily understood history of their faith (1:1-4)

Theme: The worldwide religion of kindness, brotherhood, and joy brought into being through Christ

Contents:

1. Preface (1:1-4)
2. The birth, infancy, and childhood of Jesus (1:5-2:52)
3. His preparation for his ministry (3:1-4:13)
    a. John the Baptist's mission (3:1-20)
    b. Jesus' baptism, genealogy, temptation (3:21-4:13)
4. The Galilean ministry (4:14-9:50)
    a. In Nazareth and Capernaum, the calling of the disciples, miracles of healing (4:14-6:16)
    b. The sermon on the plain (6:17-49)
    c. Miracles, teachings, parables (7:1-9:17)
    d. Peter's confession, the transfiguration, teachings (9:18-50)
5. On the road to Jerusalem: most of the narratives, parables, miracles, and sayings found only in Luke (9:51-19:27)
6. The ministry in Jerusalem (19:28-21:38)
7. The last hours of Jesus' life (22:1-23:56)
8. After the resurrection (24)

Introduction:

The Gospel of Luke and the Acts of the Apostles were originally a two-volume work recording the beginnings of Christianity from the birth of Jesus to Paul's arrival in Rome. A single author is believed to have written these two books because both are dedicated to a man named Theophilus and both are similar in vocabulary, style, and point of view. Though neither volume gives the author's name, it might have been Luke, a Gentile who accompanied Paul on his missionary journeys (Col 4:11,14; 2 Tim 4:11) and whose travel diary may be preserved in the so-called "we"-sections of Acts. If Luke is indeed the author, he is probably the only Gentile who made a major contribution to the Bible.

Of the approximately 1,200 verses in this Gospel, some 350 are derived from Mark's total of 660 verses. About 325 verses are from Q, the hypothetical source from which Matthew and Luke derived the sayings of Jesus. Luke's remaining 525 or so verses are peculiar to this Gospel and contain many of the passages that give it its unique quality and emphasis. Among the events found only in Luke are those concerning: Jesus' birth (1:5-2:52); his sermon at Nazareth (4:16-30); Martha and Mary (10:38-42); Zacchaeus (19:1-10); the penitent thief (23:40-43); the travelers to Emmaus (24:13-35); and the ascension (24:50-53). Only Luke contains the parables of the Good Samaritan, the Friend at Midnight, the Lost Coin, the Prodigal Son, and the Rich Man and Lazarus (10:29-37; 11:5-8; 15:8-10, 11-32; 16:19-31).

The distinctive features of this Gospel reflect the author's character and outlook and also his care to remove any possible suspicion on the part of intelligent Gentiles that Christianity threatened the state. Chief among this book's characteristics are: (1) its high literary quality; (2) its clarity

The Gospel According to Luke

and logical sequence; (3) the universality of its message; (4) its note of compassion for the poor, the suffering, the outcasts; (5) the prominence it gives to women; (6) its emphasis on prayer; (7) its undercurrent of defense against suspicion on the part of Roman officials; and (8) its atmosphere of joy.

This Gospel is a work of history, but, as it was written by a gifted writer of keen sensibility, it did not become a dull chronicle. Using good Greek and presenting his materials in an orderly fashion, Luke infused charm and color into his narrative and depicted characters in a lively, appealing way, making this the most readable of the Gospels.

Luke's preoccupation with the worldwide aspect of Christianity, so dramatically recorded in Acts, is first encountered in the genealogy of Jesus. Instead of beginning with the descent of Jesus from Abraham, as does the genealogy in Matthew, Luke traces the ancestry of Jesus back to Adam the father of all men. From the angel's announcement of the good news of great joy "to all people" (2:10) to Christ's command to preach "in his name to all nations" (24:47), Luke stresses the universal message of Christianity.

Linked with this message for all peoples is his preoccupation with human happiness and welfare. Tenderness and compassion are so prominent in Luke's portrait of Jesus that Dante called this evangelist, "the scribe of the gentleness of Christ." The humanitarian theme is first expressed in Mary's song.

> "He has put down the mighty from their thrones,
> and exalted those of low degree;
> he has filled the hungry with good things."
>
> Luke 1:52-53

Later this theme is expanded when Jesus, in words quoted from Isaiah 61:1, states that God has sent him to

" . . . preach good news to the poor.
He has sent me to proclaim release to the captives
and recovering of sight to the blind,
to set at liberty those who are oppressed . . . ."

Luke 4:18

More women appear in this Gospel than in any other. Only Luke records incidents concerning Elizabeth, Anna, the widow at Nain, the sinful woman, certain events involving Martha and Mary, and some of the stories about the mother of Jesus. All these narratives take for granted the dignity and importance of women.

Luke's emphasis on prayer is evident in his references to Jesus praying (3:21; 6:12; 9:18,29; 11:1). Luke alone records the prayer from the cross, "Father, forgive them; for they know not what they do" (23:34).

The author aimed, in this book and in Acts, to win for Christianity the recognition and privileges accorded to Judaism under Roman law. He produced evidence to show that the new religion was faithful to Judaism, with its synagogues, scriptures, and Temple (2:22-39; 4:16-22; 19:45-48). Moreover, he recorded examples of Jesus and his followers living within the framework of Roman law and custom (5:27-32; 7:2-9) and instances of Roman officials declaring that Jesus was innocent of lawbreaking (23:1-4,15,20-24,47).

Finally, an atmosphere of good tidings, joy, and the power of the Holy Spirit illuminates this Gospel. Such words as "gladness," "joy," and "rejoice" occur nearly twice as often in Luke as in the other three Gospels combined.

* * * *

St. Francis of Assisi may have been the first person to create for Christmas a nativity tableau called a *crèche*, "crib,"

The National Galleries of Scotland, Edinburgh

Christ in the House of Mary and Martha -- Vermeer (c. 1654)

Vermeer interprets the hushed moment when Martha, having voiced her complaint to Jesus, pauses while he points to Mary, who knows that "man shall not live by bread alone, but by every word that proceeds from the mouth of God."

or *presepio*, "manger." In 1223, he decorated a stable and used live animals and representations of people to portray the scene narrated in Luke 2:1-16. Here he celebrated Mass and preached throughout the Christmas season.

* * * *

Jesse, the father of King David, is listed in both Luke 3:32 and Matthew 1:6 as an ancestor of Jesus. For this reason, a so-called "Jesse tree" is a representation of the descent of Jesus from the royal family of Israel. A Jesse tree portrayed in stained glass in churches and cathedrals is called a Jesse window.

* * * *

The "lucky dip" method of finding a Biblical verse applicable to one's present need may have bizarre results. Using this method of opening the Bible at random and pointing with closed eyes, an old woman is alleged to have happened upon Matthew 27:5, "he [Judas] went and hanged himself." She tried again only to find Luke 10:37, "Go and do likewise."

* * * *

The names of the disciples, as recorded in Luke 6:14-16, all appear in this jingle:

> This is the way the disciples run:
> Peter and Andrew, James and John,
> Philip and Bartholomew,
> Thomas next and Matthew, too,
> James "the less" and Judas (the greater),
> Simon the Zealot, and Judas, the traitor.

The Gospel According to John

An Interpretation of the Mystery and Meaning of Christ

Position: Fourth Gospel, 4th book of the New Testament

Date: Between A.D. 85 and 100

Sources: The Gospels of Mark and Luke; oral and written eyewitness testimony; other Church traditions

Author: Traditionally identified as the apostle John, but now thought by most scholars to be one of John's disciples

Style: Sublime, moving, vivid, with concrete details, but having a limited vocabulary and monotonous syntax

Written for: Christians of a predominantly Greek city, probably Ephesus

Purpose: " . . . written that you may believe that Jesus is the Christ, the Son of God, and that believing you may have life in his name" (20:31)

Theme: The belief that "In the beginning was the Word, and the Word was with God, and the Word was God . . . . And the Word became flesh and dwelt among us, full of grace and truth; we have beheld his glory, glory as of the only Son from the Father." (1:1-18)

Contents:

1. Prelude (1)
    a. The eternal origin and divine nature of Christ (1:1-18)
    b. Early witnesses to Jesus as the Son of God (1:19-51)
2. The seven "signs" manifesting Christ's power and glory, with their subsequent events and discourses (2-12)

    Sign 1—Water turned into wine at Cana (2:1-12)
    a. Cleansing of the Temple (2:13-25)
    b. Nicodemus and the discourse on the new birth (3:1-21)
    c. John the Baptist's witness to Jesus (3:22-36)
    d. The Samaritan woman and Jesus' claim to be the Messiah (4:1-42)

    Sign 2—The healing of the nobleman's son (4:43-54)

    Sign 3—The healing of the lame man at the Pool of Bethzatha (5)

    Sign 4—The feeding of the five thousand (6:1-14)

    Sign 5—The walking on the water (6:15-21)
    a. Discourse on the bread of life (6:22-71)
    b. Jesus at the Feast of Tabernacles (7-8)

    Sign 6—Restoration of sight to a man born blind (9)
    a. Discourse on the Good Shepherd (10:1-21)
    b. Jesus at the Feast of Dedication (10:22-42)

    Sign 7—The raising of Lazarus (11)
    a. The anointing of Jesus at Bethany (12:1-11)
    b. The triumphal entry into Jerusalem (12:12-19)
    c. Jesus and the Gentiles (12:20-36)
    d. Jewish unbelief (12:37-50)

3. Christ's fuller revelation of himself to his disciples (13-17)

a. The last supper (13:1-30)
   b. Farewell discourses (13:31-16:33)
   c. His prayer for the Church (17)
4. The final revelation of Christ's glory (18-20)
   a. His arrest and trials (18:1-19:16)
   b. His crucifixion and burial (19:17-42)
   c. His resurrection (20)
5. Epilogue (21)
   a. The risen Christ with his disciples in Galilee (21:1-19)
   b. Attestation of the Gospel (21:20-25)

Introduction:

John's Gospel is unique among the four in that it reflects a longer development in Christian thought and experience than do the other three so-called Synoptic Gospels. In the 3rd century, the Greek theologian Clement of Alexandria wrote, "Last of all John, perceiving that the bodily, literal facts had been set forth in the other Gospels, with the inspiration of the Spirit composed a spiritual gospel." This does not mean that the Fourth Gospel is unhistorical, for it draws from the same oral tradition underlying the other three. But where they record Jesus' words and deeds, John goes behind the external facts to their ultimate meaning and meditates upon the divine origin and nature of Christ. The Fourth Gospel is not so much a record of facts as a testimony to religious experience and spiritual truth. In its attempt to impart a more confident and truer faith in Christ and a closer communion with him, this Gospel delves more deeply into the inner life of Jesus than do the other Gospels.

John, following his own largely independent course, uses sources unknown to the other evangelists. His chronology differs from Mark's at three points. He reports that the ministry of Jesus overlapped that of John the Baptist, while Mark states that Jesus began to preach only after John's imprisonment. The Fourth Gospel mentions three Passovers during the ministry of Jesus, the first of which was attended by him (2:13; 6:4; 11:55), while Mark apparently reports a shorter ministry. In John's Gospel, the last supper takes place on the evening before the Passover (13:1,29; 18:28; 19:14), but in Mark, it is the Passover meal.

Other differences between the Synoptic Gospels and John underline the uniqueness of the Fourth Gospel. In the Synoptics, Galilee is the chief scene of Jesus' ministry; in John, events that took place in Judea and particularly in Jerusalem are prominent. While the miracles are used in the Synoptics largely to express the compassion of Jesus, in John they become dramatic "signs" of God's power working through Jesus to give, sustain, and heal man's life. They show that people who were in the presence of Jesus felt the reality of God's power (2:11).

Instead of the parables found in the Synoptics, the Fourth Gospel has figurative discourses of "the vine" (15:1-8) and "the Good Shepherd" (10:1-18). The epigrammatic sayings characteristic of Jesus' teaching as recorded in the Synoptics reappear in John in the midst of such elaborate philosophical discourses that their original, pithy quality is largely obscured. The practical teachings of Jesus in the Synoptics become abstract in John and involve the mystery of Christ's person.

John's portrayal of Jesus conveys both lowliness and sublimity. But Jesus' divine nature tends to overshadow his humanity, and the human traits so vividly reported in the Synoptics are somewhat less prominent in the Fourth Gospel. The Synoptics note a deepening understanding by Jesus of his mission and the growing realization of his disciples that he is the Messiah. The Fourth Gospel eliminates this development and, at the very beginning of the ministry, records the cry of John the Baptist, "I have seen and have borne witness that this is the Son of God" (1:34).

Though John's Gospel omits such outstanding events as the birth, baptism, temptation, and transfiguration of Jesus and his blessing and distribution of the bread and wine at the last supper, it introduces new personalities and events. Among these are: the miracle at Cana, the discourses with Nicodemus and with the woman of Samaria, the visits to Jerusalem, the healing of the lame man at the Pool of Bethzatha, the restoring of sight to the man born blind, and the raising of Lazarus. John also adds new information about: Mary the mother of Jesus, John the Baptist, Mary Magdalene, Peter, Caiaphas, Pilate, and Judas Iscariot.

Tradition names the apostle John, the son of Zebedee, as the author of this Gospel and points to Ephesus as the city where it was written, but internal and external evidence weaken this theory of authorship. Among the arguments against John's authorship are the following: (1) The appendix, in endorsing this Gospel (21:24), makes no claim to apostolic authorship. (2) In the Gospels and Acts, John the son of Zebedee is portrayed as a man of fiery temper, ambitious to be first in Christ's kingdom, and a supporter of the Jews. This Gospel, however, breathes a spirit of love and brotherhood and indicates a bias against the Jews.

The extremely complex problem of authorship has been dealt with in innumerable articles and books. Some scholars attribute this Gospel to a disciple of the apostle John or to a certain John, the Elder of Ephesus mentioned by Bishop Papias. Whoever the author was, he clearly possessed, next to Paul, one of the most remarkable and original minds of the early Church. He understood and was able to portray Jesus as a historical person and at the same time, by revealing the inner meaning of his life, to present him as the eternal Lord ever abiding with his faithful people.

* * * *

Under layers of rubble beneath the present convent of Notre Dame de Sion in Jerusalem, archaeologists recently discovered a pavement measuring 165 by 150 feet. The three-foot-square limestone blocks of this pavement, worn smooth by traffic, are believed to mark the site of the courtyard in the fortress of Antonia where Pilate's military headquarters were located. If this is true, this pavement, apart from the Temple enclosure, is the only archaeologically authentic Gospel site in Jerusalem. In John 19:13 this courtyard is identified as, "the Pavement, in Hebrew Gabbatha," where Pilate presented his thorn-crowned prisoner to the crowd. Some of the paving stones are marked with the Roman soldiers' game of *basilikos*, "royal," which may have suggested to them the form of Jesus' mocking. This courtyard must once have echoed to the cry, "Crucify him!"

* * * *

According to John 10:23, Jesus, during his winter visit to Jerusalem, walked "in the temple in the portico of Solomon." Though this portico, which was constructed by King Herod during his elaborate rebuilding of the Temple, was destroyed by the Romans in A.D. 70, some idea of its beauty may be gained from a limestone ossuary now in the British Museum, London. This small casket, like those used for the bones of the dead in the period just before the fall of Jerusalem, was discovered near that city in 1870. Surely, the handsome arcade of eight arches and Corinthian-type capitals all carved on the lid of this ossuary represent a well-known structure. Is it not likely that they represent the Temple portico?

The Acts of the Apostles

The Only Contemporary History of Early Christianity

Position: Fifth book of the New Testament

Date: Between A.D. 75 and 100

Sources: The author's personal knowledge, also facts he learned from others; oral and written material concerning the Jerusalem and Antioch churches

Author: Probably, the author of the Third Gospel

Written for: Christians living in such cities as Rome, Antioch, Ephesus; Roman officials, especially Theophilus

Purpose: To commend Christianity to the Gentile world

Theme: The triumphant advance of the Church, through the power of the Holy Spirit, from Jerusalem to Rome

Contents:

1. The period of Church expansion dominated by Peter (1-12)
   a. Origin of the Jerusalem church (1-7)

b. Spread of the gospel as a result of persecution (8:1-9:32)
      1) Philip's missionary work (8)
      2) Conversion of Saul of Tarsus (9:1-25)
      3) Saul's first visit to Jerusalem (9:26-31)
   c. Expansion from Palestine to Syria (9:32-12:25)
      1) Peter's miracles at Lydda and Joppa, and his baptism of Gentiles at Caesarea (9:32-11:18)
      2) The church in Antioch (11:19-30)
      3) Herod's persecution of the Church, death of James, imprisonment of Peter (12)
2. Paul's labors to bring the gospel to the Gentile world (13-28)
   a. First missionary journey to Cyprus and Asia Minor (13-14)
   b. The apostolic council concerning the admission of Gentiles to the Church (15:1-35)
   c. Second missionary journey to Asia Minor, Macedonia, Achaia (15:36-18:22)
   d. Third missionary journey to Asia Minor, Ephesus, Macedonia, Achaia; return to Jerusalem (18:23-21:17)
   e. Paul, a prisoner (21:18-28:31)
      1) In Jerusalem (21:18-23:35)
      2) In Caesarea (24-26)
      3) En route to Rome (27:1-28:15)
      4) In Rome (28:16-31)

Introduction:

The Acts of the Apostles was undoubtedly written by the same author who wrote the Gospel of Luke. He dedicated it, like his "first book," to Theophilus (Lk 1:1-4, cf. Acts 1:1-2). The entire work presents a history of the origins of Christianity, beginning with the life and ministry of Jesus Christ and ending about A.D. 63 with Paul's proclamation of the new faith in the imperial city of Rome.

Acts is less concerned with the lives and acts of the various apostles than with the expansion of the Church under the guidance and inspiration of the Holy Spirit. Peter and Paul are the only apostles who figure to any extent, the others being little more than names. Even the deeds of Peter and Paul become incidental to the onward sweep of Christianity under the dominance of the Holy Spirit. Acts 2:1-12 records the coming of the Spirit to the Church and thereafter this history attributes the success of the Christian mission to men "full of the Holy Spirit" (7:55). As Luke's first volume is the Gospel of the Son, his second might be named the Gospel of the Holy Spirit.

The Holy Spirit is mentioned some fifty times in Acts. This emphasis on the Spirit is also characteristic of Luke's Gospel, which contains more references to the Holy Spirit than any of the other three Gospels. This detail gives additional support to the theory that Acts and Luke were written by the same author.

Acts is permeated by the same joyous atmosphere that illuminates Luke's Gospel, an atmosphere clearly evident in the frequently recurring words, *rejoice, gladness,* and *joy.* It contains such stories as that of Paul and Silas singing hymns during their imprisonment at Philippi—stories that convey an indomitable enthusiasm.

Acts continues Luke's defense of Christianity. It proves that, far from being subversive, Peter, Paul, and their associates not only cooperated with the authorities but were frequently declared by Roman officials to be innocent of the charges brought against them. Luke's many references to civil and military authorities by name or exact title and the large part of his history devoted to a virtual catalogue of Paul's acquittals (16-28) show that he attached great importance to a good relationship between Christianity and the state.

Human brotherhood and the universal scope of Christianity, both prominent in Luke's Gospel, are dramatized in Acts in the story of Pentecost (2:1-21) and later episodes. In fact, Peter's baptism of the Gentile centurion Cornelius (10:1-11:18) and Paul's statement at Antioch of Pisidia, " . . . behold we turn to the Gentiles" (13:46), are used in this history as turning points in the Church's onward march toward universal brotherhood.

Outstanding features of Acts are: (1) its gallery of vivid portraits; (2) its wealth of local color and geographical references; (3) its collection of speeches comprising nearly a quarter of the book; (4) its summary statements; and (5) a travel diary, probably Luke's.

Despite their widely different human traits and their unmistakable individuality, the first Christians are portrayed with a striking family resemblance. Luke shows them bound together in fellowship and acting under the power of the Holy Spirit while they coped with the problems of the real world. Their failures and the clash of their personalities are candidly recorded. Besides the dominant figures of Peter and Paul, Luke sketches lifelike portraits of such people as: Barnabas, Ananias and Sapphira, Gamaliel, Stephen, Philip, Cornelius, Lydia, the jailer at Philippi, Aquila and Priscilla, the town clerk at Ephesus, Julius the centurion.

Acts conveys a vivid and authentic picture of life in the 1st century, touching on such aspects as: poverty in Jerusalem, religious persecution, civil disturbance, travel, commerce and shipping, shipwreck, the silversmiths' monopoly at Ephesus, the philosophers of Athens, legal actions. Throughout the book, the geographical references are usually exact.

The National Gallery, London

Christ Blesses the Children -- Nicholas Maes (c. 1665)

People often bring their children to a great man when he comes to town. Jesus will draw from this event one of his most profound teachings. Mark 10:13-16

The speeches in Acts follow a common literary practice of ancient historians who put words in the mouths of their heroes to increase the dramatic effect. Though the speeches attributed to such people as Peter, Gamaliel, Stephen, Cornelius, and Paul cannot be taken as verbatim reports, undoubtedly, they convey an accurate picture of early Christian beliefs. Moreover, these speeches, with their eloquence and drama, enliven the narrative and serve both to characterize the people involved and to explain the issues.

Basically, Acts is a compilation of carefully chosen episodes woven into a consecutive narrative. Luke compresses parts of his voluminous information into brief summaries, using these to make transitions and to indicate the passage of time. The significant days following the ascension are summarized as follows: "All these with one accord devoted themselves to prayer, together with the women and Mary the mother of Jesus, and with his brothers" (1:14). Other summaries include: 2:42-47, 4:32-35; 5:12-16,42; 6:7; 8:1-3; 9:31; 12:24.

The sections of Acts expressed in the first person plural, the so-called "we"-passages or travel diary (16:10-17; 20:5-15; 21:1-18; 27:1-28:16), are written in the same style as the rest of the book. They appear to have been written by a companion of Paul who remained in Caesarea during the apostle's imprisonment there and was shipwrecked with him on the voyage to Rome. This companion is usually thought to be Luke because Paul's allusions to him in the letters correspond to the "we"-passages.

If Luke was as closely connected with leaders of the early Church as the "we"-passages indicate, the historical value of Acts is very great. At times Luke may have sacrificed accuracy to effect and he may have made errors in details, but a comparison of Acts with Paul's letters, with geographical facts, and with contemporary inscriptions and docu-

The Acts of the Apostles

ments bears out the trustworthiness of Luke's work. Far from being a historical romance like some of the later apocryphal "Acts," the Acts of the Apostles is clearly reliable history.

* * * *

The famine relief fund collected by the Christians of Antioch is the first recorded instance of organized, voluntary aid for disaster victims. Paul and Barnabas took this money to the church in Judea where many were hungry because of the severe crop failure of A.D. 46 (Acts 11:27-30).

* * * *

Abraham Lincoln and his cabinet were one day discussing what motto to engrave on the new paper money. After several suggestions had been made, Lincoln, with wry humor, proposed Peter's words, "Silver and gold have I none; but such as I have give I thee" (Acts 3:6,KJV).

* * * *

Simon, the magician of Samaria, envious of Peter and John because of the miracles they performed, tried to buy from them some of their spiritual power. "Your silver perish with you," replied Peter, "because you thought you could obtain the gift of God with money!" (Acts 8:20). From Simon's name comes the term *simony* for the buying and selling of sacred things or ecclesiastical positions.

The Letter of Paul to the Romans

Paul's Answer to the Question "What is Christianity?"

Position: Sixth book of the New Testament

Date: Between A.D. 53 and 58

Author: Paul

Style: Fresh, vigorous, solemn, well-written, carefully organized

Written to: Members of the church in Rome

Purpose: To introduce Paul's gospel of salvation

Theme: The abounding grace and "love of God in Christ Jesus our Lord" for both Jews and Gentiles

Contents:

1. Introduction (1:1-15)
2. The gospel of salvation (1:16-4:25)
   a. Statement of theme (1:16-17)
   b. The universal need of salvation because of humanity's sin and guilt (1:18-3:20)
   c. The grace of God that brings deliverance through Christ to all who believe (3:21-31)
   d. Testimony from the Scriptures (4)
3. The new life in Christ (5-8)
   a. Its character of peace, faith, hope, love, and victory over sin (5)
   b. Deliverance from sin and the Law in the life under grace (6-7)

The Letter of Paul to the Romans

   c. Summary of Paul's message: freedom, power, present help, and future glory are assured "for those who are in Christ Jesus" (8:1-30)
   d. Hymn to God's love—"in all these things we are more than conquerors through him who loved us" (8:31-39)
4. Answer to the problem of Israel's destiny—God's ultimate mercy on both Jew and Gentile (9-11)
5. Christian living and the law of love (12:1-15:13)
   a. Basic attitudes (12:1-8)
   b. Right relations (12:9-13:14)
   c. Respecting the views of others (14:1-15:6)
   d. Conclusion and prayer (15:7-13)
6. Postscript (15:14-33)
7. A letter introducing Phoebe, greetings, doxology (16)

Introduction:

Romans, the longest and most important of the New Testament letters, is Paul's most carefully prepared and written letter. In it he makes a profoundly moving statement of the essentials of Christian faith. According to the English scholar and theologian, Charles H. Dodd, Romans is "the first great work of Christian theology" and in Western Christendom "there is probably no other single writing so deeply embedded in our heritage of thought."

Paul wrote this letter probably at Corinth in the home of Gaius (Rom 16:23; 1 Cor 1:14), or at the nearby port of Cenchreae (16:1). For the past six or seven years he had traveled through Asia Minor, Macedonia, Illyricum, and Greece, establishing churches in the great cities and seaports. Now, at the end of his third missionary journey, he looked forward to longer journeys, planning to go to Rome and from there to carry the gospel westward into Spain. Before all this, however, as he explained to the Romans, his first duty was to take the relief funds collected from his Greek churches to the poor in the mother church in Jerusalem (15: 23-28; Acts 20:2-3). Written at the height of Paul's career, after years of successful missionary work and on the eve of what he confidently expected would be greater labors, this letter summarizes his deepest religious insights. Romans, however, proved to be the last letter he wrote as an active missionary and as a free man.

A variety of reasons must have prompted Paul to write Romans. First, he wanted to introduce himself to the Christians of the imperial city and announce his forthcoming visit to them. For this purpose a brief letter would have sufficed. The Roman church had been in existence for some twenty or so years, founded possibly by "visitors from Rome, both Jews and proselytes" (Acts 2:10) who had first learned about Christianity on a visit to Jerusalem at Pentecost. In succeeding years the Roman church had become so influential that Paul said of it, "your faith is proclaimed in all the world" (1:8). Yet, as an apostle he felt his responsibility "to lead to faith and obedience men of all nations, yourselves among them, you who have heard the call and belong to Jesus Christ" (1:5-6, NEB). He hoped that his letter and his presence among them would "impart to you some spiritual gift to strengthen you" (1:11). Furthermore, he must have thought that this church, which he described as "full of goodness, filled with all knowledge, and able to instruct one another" (15:14), was capable of understanding his deepest thoughts. In other cities he had been misunderstood or criticized. Here he hoped to find intelligent response to his teachings and support for his projected journey to Spain. Beneath these motives may have been his desire to leave with a strong, alert church a carefully reasoned, comprehensive statement of the nature of his faith before again facing the dangers of missionary journeys.

In the last chapter of Romans Paul sends a surprising number of greetings to friends. But how did he have so many in a city he had not yet visited? According to one hypothesis, this last chapter may originally have been a separate letter of introduction for Phoebe, a deaconess of Cenchreae, who was traveling, not to Rome, but to Ephesus. Paul had recently spent three years in Ephesus and, when last heard from, Prisca (Priscilla) and Aquila were living there (16:3-4, cf. Acts 18:18-19; 1 Cor 16:19). The twenty-six named friends could be Ephesians Paul had known during his three-year sojourn. The short letter with its concluding doxology was probably added to Romans when this great Christian document was copied for the church at Ephesus.

Paul's message in the main part of Romans was "the saving power of God for everyone who has faith—the Jew first, but the Greek also—because here is revealed God's way of righting wrong" (1:16 NEB). Paul showed that by faith in Christ people are freed from bondage to sin and from the external restrictions of the Law so that henceforth they live a new life in the Spirit, a life in right relationship to God.

In the eighth chapter, one of the greatest in the Bible, Paul sums up his messages in a series of affirmations. "For the law of the Spirit of life in Christ Jesus has set me free from the law of sin and death" (8:2). "For . . . those who live according to the Spirit set their minds on the things of the Spirit. To set the mind on the flesh is death, but to set the mind on the Spirit is life and peace" (8:5-6). "For all who are led by the Spirit of God are sons of God" (8:14). "We know that in everything God works for good with those who love him, who are called according to his purpose" (8:28). "If God is for us, who is against us?" (8:31). "For I am sure that neither death, nor life, nor angels, nor principalities, nor things present, nor things to come, nor powers, nor height, nor depth, nor anything else in all creation, will be able to separate us from the love of God in Christ Jesus our Lord" (8:38-39).

* * * *

One day in the year 387, as Augustine wept under a fig tree because he felt hopelessly entangled in his doubts and the sins of his pleasure-loving life, he heard a sweet voice singing, "Take up and read." Obeying the repeated command, Augustine opened the Bible and read, "Let us conduct ourselves becomingly . . . not in reveling and drunkenness, not in debauchery and licentiousness, not in quarreling and jealousy. But put on the Lord Jesus Christ, and make no provision for the flesh, to gratify its desires" (Rom 13:13-14). Augustine felt that this message was meant especially for him. It illuminated his heart with a great light, bringing serenity, banishing doubt, and finally converting him to Christianity. From that hour he devoted his great abilities and intellect single-mindedly to God's service.

The First Letter of Paul to the Corinthians

A Practical Application of Christian Teachings to First-Century Church Life

Position: Seventh book of the New Testament

Date: Between A.D. 53 and 58

Author: Paul

The First Letter of Paul to the Corinthians

Style:	Direct, informal, personal, with beauty of cadence especially in 13:1-13 and 15:42-58
Written to:	Members of the church in Corinth
Purpose:	To help the Corinthians solve their problems
Theme:	The application of Christian values and moral principles

Contents:

1. Salutation (1:1-9)
2. Admonition to unity in the face of disagreements (1:10-4:21)
3. Comments on the moral difficulties reported to him (5-6)
   a. An instance of immorality (5)
   b. Lawsuits between Christians (6:1-8)
   c. Warnings against immorality (6:9-20)
4. Paul's answers to questions asked of him (7-15)
   a. Marriage and celibacy (7)
   b. The eating of meat consecrated to idols (8-10)
   c. The veiling of women in church (11:1-16)
   d. The celebration of the Lord's Supper (11:17-34)
   e. Spiritual gifts; the hymn to love; the conduct of worship (12-14)
5. The significance of the resurrection (15)
6. Final message and autograph greeting (16)

Introduction:

Paul was living temporarily in Ephesus when members of Chloe's household arrived from Corinth with disturbing news. They reported that in his absence dissident factions were undermining the church he had founded. Moreover, a conspicuous instance of immorality and a number of lawsuits between church members showed that Christian standards of living were deteriorating.

At about the same time, Paul received a letter from the Corinthians asking for his advice on a variety of questions. Should Christians refrain from marriage in view of the expected early end of the world? Should a Christian divorce a pagan spouse? Was meat offered to idols unfit for Christians to eat? Should women be veiled in church? How should the Lord's Supper be celebrated? Which is more important: preaching, healing, working miracles, prophesying, or speaking in tongues? Is there really a resurrection from the dead? Such problems gave Paul an opportunity to explain the essential meaning of the gospel.

Corinth had been an unlikely place for Christianity to gain a foothold. It was a busy commercial center, more important than Athens at this time. Situated on an isthmus, it was a maritime crossroads dominating the commerce of Greece as well as of the entire eastern Mediterranean. Though pagan influences were strong in this pleasure-loving, licentious city, the church Paul founded had flourished. If it were to survive its present crisis, however, it needed Paul's insight in relating its unique problems to the Christian message as a whole.

This letter is not a theological treatise, as parts of Romans appear to be, but a practical application of Christian doctrine to urgent local problems. It is valuable, both as a picture of life in a first-century church, and as an expression of Paul's understanding of the meaning of the gospel.

Paul rebuked the Corinthians for their party quarrels in which members were allied exclusively with Apollos, or himself, or Peter, or some other human leader. He demanded that the member guilty of incest be disciplined; that Christians cease taking lawsuits (between themselves) to pagan courts; and that immorality be banished. His belief in the imminent return of Christ and the end of the age influenced his advice about marriage. Though he saw no objection to eating meat sacrificed to idols, he urged liberal-minded Christians to respect the scruples of others. He said that, in accordance with the custom of the time, women must be veiled in church, and everyone must be reverent at the Lord's Supper. Of the many spiritual gifts, including prophecy, visions, and speaking in "various kinds of tongues," Paul declared that the most valuable of all is love. To those at Corinth who denied the resurrection of the dead, he stated his faith. His declaration is the oldest surviving record of Christ's resurrection, having been written only twenty-five years after the event itself and long before the accounts in the Gospels (1 Cor 15:3-9). Paul's narrative of the last supper (1 Cor 11:23-26) is also the oldest surviving written record of that event.

This letter contains some of Paul's most inspired utterances. According to Erasmus, "Paul thunders and lightens and speaks sheer flame." Outstanding portions include: his discussion of spiritual gifts (12); the exquisite hymn to Christian love, beginning, "If I speak in the tongues of men and of angels, but have not love . . . " (13); his statement concerning the value of prophecy (14); and the magnificent passage on immortality, which includes the sentence, "For as in Adam all die, so also in Christ shall all be made alive" (15:22). This passage ends in exaltation:

> The sting of death is sin, and the
> power of sin is the law. But thanks
> be to God, who gives us the victory
> through our Lord Jesus Christ.
> 1 Corinthians 15:56-57

* * * *

Anne Hutchinson, a brilliant and very kind woman was banished from the Massachusetts Bay Colony in 1637 for preaching what the Reverend John Cotton and Governor John Winthrop considered heresy. Her judges ruled that Paul's words to the ancient Corinthians applied to Anne: "The women should keep silence in the churches. For they are not permitted to speak, but should be subordinate, as even the law says" (1 Cor 14:34). "What law?" objected Anne. Her judges, unprepared for her quick defense, fell back upon the Fifth Commandment about honoring one's parents and ruled that she had dishonored the "fathers" of the colony by talking too much. (Actually, the "law" Paul referred to was probably Genesis 3:16.) Anne and her family, after her banishment, settled at what is now Pelham Bay Park, New York City, where they died in the Indian massacre of 1643.

* * * *

In his four presidential inaugurations, Franklin D. Roosevelt used a Dutch Bible, printed in 1687, that contained the Roosevelt family records from the beginning of the 18th century. This is the oldest of the known inaugural Bibles and the only one in a modern foreign language. While taking his oath of office, President Roosevelt rested his hand on Paul's hymn to love in 1 Corinthians 13.

The Second Letter of Paul to the Corinthians

Paul's Account of His Life and Faith

Position: Eighth book of the New Testament

The Second Letter of Paul to the Corinthians

Date: Between A.D. 53 and 58

Author: Paul

Style: Intense, personal, moving

Written to: The church in Corinth

Purposes: To defend Paul's authority and reestablish good relations with the church he had founded

Theme: "If any one is in Christ, he is a new creation" (5:17)

Contents:

1. Paul's letter of thanksgiving after receiving good news from Corinth (1-9)
   a. Salutation and thanksgiving (1:1-11)
   b. His relations with the church in Corinth (1:12-2:13)
   c. His apostolic ministry (2:14-6:13)
   d. A disconnected unit, possibly a fragment from an earlier letter, warning against associating with immoral people (6:14-7:1)
   e. His joy at the restoration of good relations with Corinth (7:2-16)
   f. His collection for the Jerusalem church (8-9)
2. Paul's "painful" letter (10-13)
   a. Introduction (10:1-6)
   b. Denial of charges made by his enemies (10:7-11:15)
   c. His self-defense (11:16-12:13)
   d. Plans for his third visit to Corinth (12:14-13:10)
   e. Farewell and exhortation (13:11-13)

Introduction:

In addition to 1 and 2 Corinthians, there is evidence that Paul wrote two other letters to the Christians of Corinth.

The first of these, written before 1 Corinthians, is mentioned in 1 Corinthians 5:9: "I wrote you in my letter not to associate with immoral men."

The text of 2 Corinthians also contains a reference to an earlier letter, in this case one written "out of much affliction and anguish of heart and with many tears" (2:4). This "painful" letter which, because of its tone, cannot be 1 Corinthians, may have been sent between 1 and 2 Corinthians. It thus becomes apparent that Paul wrote a series of four letters: one warning about immoral men, 1 Corinthians, the "painful" letter, and finally 2 Corinthians.

Have the warning letter and the "painful" letter been lost? Some scholars think that, in view of the lack of continuity in 2 Corinthians, it may contain parts of both of these earlier letters. It would thus be a collection of three of Paul's letters to this unruly community of Christians. A fragment of the warning letter probably survives as 2 Corinthians 6:14-7:1. These six verses abruptly break into Paul's sequence of thought and deal with relations with unbelievers. The most memorable line in the inserted fragment is the statement, "For we are the temple of the living God" (6:16).

The "painful" letter could be the reproachful, indignant message of 2 Corinthians 10-13. These four chapters are far from the mood of relief and gratitude that characterizes the first nine chapters of 2 Corinthians. Because "superlative apostles" (11:5) had gone to Corinth and had tried to undermine Paul's influence there, he defended himself against their charges and in so doing left an invaluable record of his life, including references to the incredible dangers and sufferings he had endured as an apostle.

Paul's last surviving letter to Corinth, 2 Corinthians 1-9, is intensely personal. It was written in a mood of tenderness and reconciliation following the unhappy visit (2:1) and the controversy referred to in the "painful" letter. Paul

The Second Letter of Paul to the Corinthians

defended himself against charges made by his critics. In chapters 3 to 5, he meditated on the nature of his apostleship, saying, "We are ambassadors for Christ" (5:20). In the light of his faith, he remembered his sufferings, but was convinced that

> this slight momentary affliction is preparing
> for us an eternal weight of glory beyond all
> comparison, because we look not to the things
> that are seen but to the things that are unseen;
> for the things that are seen are transient,
> but the things that are unseen are eternal.
> 2 Corinthians 4:17-18

In brief and simple terms he explained the doctrine of the Incarnation and expressed the heart of the apostolic message, "God was in Christ reconciling the world to himself" (5:19). Paul's letter ends with a practical subject—an appeal to contribute to his fund for the relief of the poor in Jerusalem (8-9).

* * * *

Second Corinthians reveals Paul, the great apostle of the early Church as his contemporaries knew him. From Paul's spirited defense of his apostleship (2 Cor 10:1-13:10) the nature of the criticism against him becomes evident. Even his detractors had to admit "'His letters are weighty and strong'" (2 Cor 10:10), a critical estimate that Paul must have welcomed. But his critics attacked him on personal grounds, saying, "'his bodily presence is weak, and his speech of no account.'" The New English Bible renders this, "'he has no presence, and as a speaker he is beneath contempt.'" For a rather poor speaker lacking an impressive personal appearance what did not Paul accomplish!

The Letter of Paul to the Galatians

A Declaration of Christian Independence

Position: Ninth book of the New Testament

Date: Between A.D. 50 and 52 or later

Author: Paul

Style: Eloquent, impassioned, powerful

Written to: Christians converted by Paul on his first missionary journey and possibly their neighbors in North Galatia

Purposes: To defend Paul's apostleship and to assert that a Gentile can be a Christian without first becoming a Jew

Theme: "In Christ Jesus you are all sons of God, through faith" (3:26)

Contents:

1. Introduction (1:1-10)
    a. Salutation (1:1-5)
    b. Reason for the letter—the Galatian apostasy (1:6-10)
2. Paul's defense of his apostleship (1:11-2:21)
    a. His call by Christ (1:11-24)
    b. The recognition of his apostleship by the Jerusalem leaders (2:1-10)
    c. His rebuke of Peter on the Gentile issue (2:11-21)
3. Freedom in Christ compared to bondage under the Law (3-4)

The Letter of Paul to the Galatians

   a. An appeal to experience and to the Scriptures (3:1-18)
   b. The Law's true purpose—to lead men to Christ (3:19-29)
   c. "Through God you are no longer a slave but a son" (4:1-31)
4. How to live in Christian freedom (5:1-6:10)
   a. The nature of Christian liberty (5:1-12)
   b. Loving service—a manifestation of freedom (5:13-15)
   c. "Walk by the Spirit, and do not gratify the desires of the flesh" (5:16-24)
   d. Personal relationships governed by the Spirit (5:25-6:10)
5. Paul's handwritten postscript (6:11-18)

Introduction:

The situation that prompted Paul to write this letter was the arrival in the churches of Galatia of certain Jewish Christians who insisted that Christianity must remain within the framework of the Jewish Law. Contrary to Paul's teaching, the Jewish Christians told the Galatians that baptism in the name of Christ and the gift of the Spirit were not sufficient for salvation. They urged the Christian Gentiles to obey the Jewish Law, submit to circumcision, observe the obligatory Jewish feasts, and keep the Sabbath rigidly. If these teachings had been followed, Christianity would have become a mere sect within Judaism.

Paul, recognizing this teaching as a threat to his apostolic authority and also to the gospel he was preaching to the Gentiles, wrote this letter. In the first two chapters he stated historical facts to support his claim to be an apostle—facts of value in establishing the history of the primitive Church.

The following four chapters provide the key to Paul's Christian message of justification by faith in Christ alone. Paul made it clear that if the Law were binding on everyone, as the Judaizers asserted, then Christ had died in vain. But Paul was convinced that Christianity offered more than did Judaism, for he believed that Christ's death redeemed everyone, both Gentile and Jew, and that to be "in Christ" means freedom from the legal requirements of Judaism. When a person accepts Christ in faith, he or she is absolved of guilt and enters into a right relationship with God.

Some of Paul's deepest spiritual insights are expressed in Galatians. "I have been crucified with Christ; it is no longer I who live, but Christ who lives in me" (2:20). "There is neither Jew nor Greek, there is neither slave nor free, there is neither male nor female; for you are all one in Christ Jesus" (3:28). "The fruit of the Spirit is love, joy, peace, patience, kindness, goodness, faithfulness, gentleness, self-control; against such there is no law" (5:22-23).

In its own day Galatians was influential in moving Christianity out of the confines of Judaism and freeing it to be a religion for all peoples. Since Paul's time, Galatians has been the Magna Charta of Christian freedom from all forms of legalism.

* * * *

Martin Luther valued this letter above all others, because he interpreted it as an indictment against the "Judaizers" of his own day. These, he believed, were church leaders who placed "a yoke of slavery" (Gal 5:1) upon Christians by making salvation dependent on outward observances rather than on a living faith in Jesus Christ.

The Letter of Paul to the Ephesians

A Meditation on "The Household of God"

Position:	Tenth book of the New Testament
Date:	About A.D. 58 or later
Author:	Paul or possibly one of his disciples
Style:	Solemn, complex
Written for:	Ephesus and all the churches of Asia Minor
Purpose:	To explain the belief that the universal Church is the body of Christ
Theme:	The Church, in which all people will finally be united, is God's instrument for accomplishing his eternal purpose

Contents:

1. Salutation (1:1-2)
2. Doctrinal section: God's purpose to unite all things in Christ (1:3-3:21)
   a. Thanksgiving for membership in Christ (1:3-14)
   b. Prayer for understanding of salvation (1:15-19)
   c. Christ's supremacy (1:20-23)
   d. New life in Christ (2:1-18)
   e. The unity of "the household of God" (2:19-22)
   f. Paul's mission as an apostle to the Gentiles (3:1-13)
   g. Prayer and doxology (3:14-21)
3. Practical section: the Church as God's instrument for uniting all things in Christ (4:1-6:20)

a. The unity of the Church with its various gifts of the Spirit (4:1-16)
  b. The old life and the new (4:17-24)
  c. How Christians should act (4:25-5:20)
  d. Relationships in the Christian family (5:21-6:9)
  e. The whole armor of God (6:10-20)
4. Personal messages and benediction (6:21-24)

Introduction:

According to the traditional theory, Paul wrote this letter during his imprisonment in Rome and sent it to Asia Minor by Tychicus (6:21; Col 4:7-9), the messenger who also delivered Colossians and Philemon to their respective destinations. But scholars, noting that this document differs in vocabulary, style, and theological concepts from letters written unquestionably by Paul, doubt that the great apostle actually wrote it. A theory has been advanced that this letter was written by a gifted disciple, who pondered deeply his master's message as expressed in his writings and later developed Paul's religious thought to its ultimate conclusion. Ephesians, then, can be regarded as a sublime expression of Paul's faith. Charles H. Dodd values it as "the crown of Paulinism."

Ephesians may have been an encyclical, or circular letter, addressed, not exclusively to Ephesus, but to all the Gentile churches of Asia Minor. This theory is supported by evidence from the oldest and best manuscripts of Ephesians, including the Chester Beatty papyrus, the Codex Sinaiticus, and the Codex Vaticanus, in all of which the phrase "at Ephesus" (1:1, KJV) is omitted. This ancient evidence governs the translation in the Revised Standard Version. The absence of personal greetings in this letter may be explained by its encyclical character.

The Letter of Paul to the Ephesians

Ephesians meditates upon the ultimate purpose of God to reunite in Christ all of the world's discordant forces (1:9-10). After pondering upon the role of the Church in the light of this divine purpose, the writer declares that the Church is the body of Christ through which he accomplishes his work of reconciliation (1:23). The members of the Church through their love, understanding, and mutual service, can foster Christian unity and so bring harmony into a disordered world.

Among the best-known passages are: Christ and the Church (1:20-23); the unity of the Church (2:19-22; 4:1-7); the prayer that "Christ may dwell in your hearts through faith" (3:14-21); the Christian message applied to relationships in the Church (4:31-32), and in the home (5:21-6:4), "Put on the whole armor of God" (6:10-20).

In its concept of the Church as the body of Christ and in some way his incarnation in the world; in its moral demand that Christians "lead a life worthy of the calling to which you have been called" (4:1); in its summons to "be strong in the Lord" (6:10) and to stand firm against all the powers of evil; finally, in its clear teaching that faith and action are complementary aspects of the Christian life, this superb document has dominated and led Christian thought and practice for centuries.

* * * *

Because it emphasizes unity in Christ, a basic goal of the modern ecumenical movement, and because it calls on Christians "to maintain the unity of the Spirit in the bond of peace" (4:3), Ephesians has been called "the most contemporary book of the New Testament."

* * * *

If one can imagine Paul, or whoever wrote Ephesians, being interviewed today, the questions and answers might go like this:

Reporter, "Why did you write in Ephesians 5:22, 'Wives be subject to your husbands'? Women have been blaming you for that for centuries!"

Paul, "You are taking the line out of its context. If you read the whole passage, you will see that I was talking about all the relationships in a Christian household, that of husband and wife as well as children and slaves. I began, 'Be subject to one another out of reverence for Christ' and addressed everyone in the household, not just the wife. I wrote this passage to enjoin mutual respect, love, and self-giving, especially in a marriage, but also in a family and in the entire household. In a household each person has a different status and each has different responsibilities. Now, next question, please."

The Letter of Paul to the Philippians

A Joyful Letter from Prison

Position: Eleventh book of the New Testament

Date: Between A.D. 53 and 63

Author: Paul

Style: Personal, warm, friendly, eloquent

Written to: Members of the church at Philippi in Macedonia

The Letter of Paul to the Philippians 67

Purposes: To thank the Philippians for their gift brought by Epaphroditus, and to share with them some of Paul's experience as a Christian

Theme: The cost in self-sacrifice and suffering of Paul's apostleship; his joy in living "in Christ"

Contents:

1. Salutation, thanksgiving, prayer (1:1-11)
2. Paul's imprisonment (1:12-26)
3. Exhortations (1:27-2:18)
    a. To live "worthy of the gospel of Christ" (1:27-30)
    b. To be "in full accord and of one mind" (2:1-4)
    c. To follow the example of Christ's humility (2:5-11)
    d. To continue in obedience (2:12-18)
4. Paul's plans for sending Timothy and Epaphroditus to Philippi (2:19-30)
5. Warnings (3:1-4:4)
    a. Against Jewish propagandists who teach contrary to Paul's experience (3:1-11)
    b. Against "perfectionism" and worldliness (3:12-21)
6. Exhortation to holy living (4:1-9)
7. Concluding thanks and salutations (4:10-23)

Introduction:

Paul wrote this informal letter while he was in Rome (Acts 28:16-20), or Caesarea (Acts 23:35), or possibly Ephesus during an unrecorded imprisonment in his two-year visit there (Acts 19:1-10).

At the time of writing he did not know "whether by life or by death" (1:20) he would be called upon to honor Christ. Nevertheless, he wrote in a mood of serene happiness and triumph. More frequently than in any of his other letters he used the words *joy* and *rejoice,* five times for the former, eight for the latter, thus displaying that mark of the saint which Baron Friedrich von Hügel, the Roman Catholic layman and Bible scholar, described as "radiance amid the storm and stress of life."

He maintained happy, confident relations with the church at Philippi, the first he had founded on the continent of Europe (Acts 16:12-40). His friends there included many besides Lydia, and the jailer, and their respective households. He described these people "as lights in the world" (2:15) and he addressed them as his "joy and crown" (4:1).

Learning that Paul was in prison, the Philippians sent a gift to him by Epaphroditus, "your messenger and minister to my need" (2:25). They planned to have their messenger remain with Paul to help him, but after Epaphroditus recovered from a grave illness, Paul sent him home with this letter of thanks.

Paul assured the Philippians that all was well with him, and that, despite his danger, his joy in Christ did not waver. After warning them against certain errors, he exhorted them to live lives worthy of Christians. Finally, with his penetrating understanding of human nature, he urged them to fill their thoughts with all that is true, honorable, pure, excellent, and worthy of praise, that the God of peace might be with them (4:8-9).

In the midst of his practical exhortations he made a remarkable statement of early Christian faith concerning Christ (2:5-11). The rhythmical cadence of this passage suggests that Paul may have been quoting from an early hymn or confession of faith. There is an echo of Second Isaiah's Servant Songs in the description of Christ's humility; "taking the form of a servant, being born in the likeness of men." In contrast to this is Christ's glory, "at the name of

The Letter of Paul to the Philippians

Jesus every knee should bow, in heaven and on earth and under the earth, and every tongue confess that Jesus Christ is Lord, to the glory of God the Father."

Believing that his life was no longer his own but belonged entirely to Christ, Paul wrote, "For me to live is Christ" (1:21). Hence, he was proud to announce himself a servant, even a slave of Christ Jesus (1:1). His imprisonment was for Christ (1:12-13) and he was confident that either by his life or by his death he would glorify his Lord (1:20). Far outweighing the loss of Paul's former worldly advantages was his gain in "knowing Christ Jesus my Lord," in sharing his sufferings, and becoming like him in his death (3:4-11). Confident that in Christ he could endure anything that life brought to him, Paul wrote,

> I have learned in whatever state I am, to be content.
> I know how to be abased, and I know how to abound;
> in any and all circumstances I have learned the secret
> of facing plenty and hunger, abundance and want.
> I can do all things in him who strengthens me.
>
> Philippians 4:11-13

* * * *

Two zealous women, leaders in the church at Philippi and fellow workers with Paul in spreading the gospel, had had a falling-out (Phil 4:2-3). This is one of the items prompting the remark that Paul takes the roof off the early Christian churches and lets us glimpse the people inside. What divided Euodia and Syntyche is not stated. Was it a genuine difference of opinion or a clash of wills and a bid for power? Whatever it was it undoubtedly threatened the church with party strife. "I entreat you Euodia and I entreat you Syntyche to agree in the Lord." With what consummate brevity Paul indicates the problem and at the same time prescribes the cure!

The Letter of Paul to the Colossians

A Challenge to Heresy

Position: Twelfth book of the New Testament

Date: Between A.D. 53 and 63

Author: Paul, although some scholars question this attribution

Style: Forceful, rugged, with long sentences and parallel clauses

Written to: Members of the church at Colossae

Purposes: To combat a heresy and give advice about living a Christian life

Theme: Christ's supremacy over all cosmic powers

Contents:

1. Salutation, thanksgiving, prayer (1:1-14)
2. Doctrinal section (1:15-2:23)
   a. The absolute supremacy of Christ (1:15-23)
   b. A reference to Paul's labors (1:24-2:7)
   c. Warning against false teaching (2:8-23)
3. A handbook of Christian morals (3:1-4:6)
   a. The real nature of the spiritual life (3:1-4)
   b. Warning against heathen vices (3:5-11)
   c. The true Christian life (3:12-17)
   d. Precepts for family life (3:18-4:1)
   e. General counsels (4:2-6)
4. Conclusion, greetings, handwritten close (4:7-18)

The Letter of Paul to the Colossians

Introduction:

Written in prison, this letter, with Philippians, Philemon, and Ephesians, belongs to the group of four so-called "prison letters." Though similar in subject matter to Ephesians, Colossians is more closely connected with Paul's short note to Philemon. Colossians and Philemon were evidently written at the same time and carried to Colossae in Asia Minor by the same messengers (4:7-9). Tychicus delivered Paul's letter to the church at Colossae while his companion Onesimus, a runaway slave from that city, was entrusted with Paul's personal note to Philemon and two other residents of Colossae.

Paul himself had never visited the Phrygian city of Colossae situated about a hundred miles east of Ephesus on the busy trade route connecting that seaport with Syria. The Colossian church had evidently been founded by Epaphras whom the apostle had met and converted during his sojourn in Ephesus. Previous to the writing of this letter, Epaphras had joined Paul and brought him news from Colossae concerning strange new doctrines that were being introduced there. Paul wrote Colossians to combat this threat to Christianity.

The new doctrines, apparently an early form of the heresy known as Gnosticism, were being advanced by heretical teachers who claimed superior, mystical knowledge and were, according to Paul, "puffed up without reason" (2:18). They were attempting to "improve" Christianity by introducing a cult of angel worship and a mixture of pagan and Jewish asceticism. Believing, as they did, that Christ was unable to free men from the hostile forces of the world, they advocated rites and magical observances to placate the cosmic powers. The aim of their asceticism was to neutralize what they regarded as the evil contamination of matter. This heresy raised the basic question: What power does Christ possess against the overwhelming forces of the world?

Paul, answering in the clear and ringing terms of a six-verse statement, declared that the whole creation is centered in Christ.

> He is the image of the invisible God, the
> first-born of creation; for in him all things
> were created, in heaven and on earth, visible
> and invisible, whether thrones or dominions or
> principalities or authorities—all things were
> created through him and for him. He is before
> all things, and in him all things hold together . . . .
>
> Colossians 1:15-20

Because Christ is the ultimate reality, the salvation he offers men is all-sufficient. Worship of Christ frees men from the need to placate the forces of this world. "For in him the whole fulness of deity dwells bodily, and you have come to fulness of life in him . . . ." (2:9-10). In 1 Corinthians 8:6, Paul had already touched on Christ's cosmic significance, but in this letter he stated it boldly and fully.

Ever the practical man of affairs, Paul not only denounced the false teachings that were leading the Colossians astray, but gave detailed advice about how to live a truly Christian life. "Set your minds on things that are above," he urged, "not on things that are on earth" (3:2). He cited "immorality, impurity, passion, evil desire, and covetousness" in which "you once walked" and the "anger, wrath, malice, slander, and foul talk" of their "old nature." Their "new nature" in Christ included: "compassion, kindness, lowliness, meekness, and patience" as well as forgiveness and, above all, love. "And whatever you do, in word or deed, do everything in the name of the Lord Jesus, giving thanks to God the Father through him" (3:17).

* * * *

How to pray and how to win "outsiders" to Christ—on these two important matters Paul tosses off the capsule advice of an expert. "Persevere in prayer, with mind awake and thankful heart" (Col 4:2, NEB). His own writing style reflects his advice about how to speak, "Let your conversation be always gracious, and never insipid; study how best to talk with each person you meet" (Col 4:6 NEB).

The First Letter of Paul to the Thessalonians

The Oldest New Testament Document Surviving in its Original Form

Position: Thirteenth book of the New Testament

Date: Between A.D. 50 and 52, during Paul's second missionary journey

Author: Paul

Style: Simple, warm, spontaneous, lively

Written for: The Christians of Thessalonica, capital of Macedonia

Purposes: To express Paul's thankfulness for the loyalty and faith of the Thessalonians, and to deal with some of their problems

Theme: How "to lead a life worthy of God, who calls you into his own kingdom and glory" (2:12)

Contents:

1. Salutation (1:1)

2. Comments on the apostolic mission at Thessalonica (1-3)
    a. Thanksgiving for their faithfulness and spiritual growth (1:2-10)
    b. Defense of his mission against Jewish critics (2:1-16)
    c. His absence from them (2:17-20)
    d. Timothy's mission and his report (3:1-10)
    e. Paul's prayer (3:11-13)
3. Concerning problems of the Thessalonians (4:1-5:22)
    a. Moral requirements of the gospel (4:1-12)
    b. The coming of the Lord (4:13-5:11)
    c. Standards to guide their Christian life (5:12-22)
4. Conclusion: prayer, precepts, benediction (5:23-28)

Introduction:

This document, probably the oldest surviving letter written by Paul, launches the great series of Christian writings that have been called the "uncut jewels" of the apostle's legacy. Not long before writing this letter, Paul, accompanied by Silas and Timothy, had spent three weeks or longer at Thessalonica proclaiming the gospel and making converts of many devout Greeks including the leading women of the city. His message was not welcomed by the Jews because they resented the fact that Paul had turned many of their Greek converts into Christians. After accusing him and his companions of sedition, the Jews instigated a riot that made it necessary for Paul to flee from the city at night (Acts 17:1-10). He journeyed to Beroea, Athens, and finally Corinth, all the while worrying about his new church at Thessalonica. Feeling that his work there was unfinished, but unable to return himself, he sent Timothy to encourage and strengthen the young church.

Timothy finally returned to Corinth bringing Paul the good news that, despite their trials, the Thessalonians remained firm in the faith and in their affection for Paul. He immediately wrote them this letter expressing his relief. "Now we live," he exclaimed, "if you stand fast in the Lord" (3:8). He thanked them for their loyalty and offered guidance in solving their problems.

In his letter he defended himself from the insinuations of his Jewish opponents by explaining his own acts and motives. In order to counteract the sexual permissiveness of the pagan environment in which his converts lived, he instructed them in Christian morals and purity of living. He calmed the fears of some who thought that certain church members who had recently died would fail to receive the blessings of the new age at the second coming of the Lord. "The dead in Christ will rise first," he assured them. "We who are alive, who are left until the coming of the Lord, shall not precede those who have fallen asleep" (4:13-18).

Some Christians had quit their work to await in idleness the second coming of Christ, an event they expected at any moment. In the interim, because their more level-headed and industrious brethren had to support them, their pagan neighbors began to ridicule the Church. Paul specifically directed the Thessalonians "to live quietly, to mind your own affairs, and to work with your hands, as we charged you; so that you may command the respect of outsiders, and be dependent on nobody" (4:11-12).

Paul's efforts to bring others to Christ and his own deep commitment to the Lord shine through this letter. Paul encourages, rebukes, and exhorts the Thessalonians, but above all he expresses his joy in his converts and his affection for them. He touches upon the great Christian truths of the early Church less as doctrines than as aspects of his own personal religion.

* * * *

Because one of the chief industries of the ancient Macedonian seaport of Thessalonica was the weaving of goat's-hair cloth, from which tents were made, Paul was able to find employment there at his trade of tentmaking (Acts 18:3). His hours, however, were evidently long, for he says, "we worked night and day, that we might not burden any of you, while we preached to you the gospel of God" (1 Thess 2:9). The lesson of his example seems to have been disregarded by some of the Thessalonians.

The Second Letter of Paul to the Thessalonians

Advice to a Young Church

Position: Fourteenth book of the New Testament

Date: Between A.D. 50 and 52

Author: Paul

Style: Simple, conversational, sometimes severe in tone

Written to: The Christians of Thessalonica

Purposes: To encourage the Thessalonians; to correct false ideas about the second coming of Christ; to instruct lazy or disorderly church members to work

Theme: The second coming of Christ

Contents:

1. Salutation, thanksgiving, and prayer (1:1-12)

2. The Lord's second coming (2)
    a. Warning against belief that this has already occurred (2:1-2)
    b. Events that will precede it (2:3-12)
    c. Exhortation to "hold to the traditions which you were taught by us" (2:13-15)
    d. Benediction (2:16-17)
3. Various counsels (3:1-15)
    a. Request for prayers (3:1-2)
    b. His confidence in them (3:3-5)
    c. Admonitions against idlers and busybodies (3:6-15)
4. Final blessing, autographed salutation (3:16-18)

Introduction:

In the brief interval between the dispatch of what is here presumed to be Paul's first message to the Thessalonians and the writing of his second letter, a disturbing situation seems to have developed in the young church. This had been caused in part by a misunderstanding of Paul's statement in his first letter that "the day of the Lord will come like a thief in the night" (1 Thess 5:2). These words alarmed many church members, making them anxious, "shaken in mind or excited" (2:2) while they awaited the imminent return of the Lord.

Paul first attempted to calm them by stating that Christ's second coming would not occur immediately. He then developed a strange theory in a passage called the Pauline Apocalypse (2:3-12). Mysterious signs, he wrote, would precede Christ's return. The "man of lawlessness," or Antichrist, who incarnates evil and is already at work, is now being restrained. But at the end of time, Antichrist, after a brief victory, will be destroyed by the Lord who will then usher in the kingdom of God. This fantastic prophecy is so unlike Paul's teachings that its authenticity is sometimes questioned, but its grandeur and philosophic depth are not unworthy of the apostle.

The idea that the present age had already ended or would soon end, as Paul noted in his First Letter to the Thessalonians, was turning some church members into idlers and beggars, to the embarrassment of their more stable and hard-working brethren. Idleness in this case was not produced by a malfunctioning of a complicated economic system, but by a misunderstanding of the Christian message combined with sheer laziness. To many pagans, Christianity seemed to foster indolence and fanaticism. Paul attacked this problem forthrightly, declaring

> If any one will not work, let him not eat.
> For we hear that some of you are living in
> idleness, mere busybodies, not doing any
> work. Now such persons we command and exhort
> in the Lord Jesus Christ to do their work in
> quietness and to earn their own living.
>
> 2 Thessalonians 3:10-12

* * * *

Paul's enemies used the trick of writing a forged letter to discredit him. In this communication he mentions such a letter "purporting to be from us" (2 Thess 2:2), which had disturbed his converts. Paul combatted his enemies' forgeries by validating with his own handwritten greeting the letters his scribes wrote at his dictation. "I, Paul, write this greeting with my own hand. This is the mark in every letter of mine; it is the way I write" (2 Thess 3:17).

The First Letter of Paul to Timothy

Advice for Church Leaders

Position: Fifteenth book of the New Testament

Date: About A.D. 100, if not by Paul.

Author: Traditionally attributed to Paul, but now often credited to a later writer

Style: Solemn, monotonous, unlike Paul's vehemence and vividness

Written to: Church leaders and the communities in their charge

Purpose: To preserve Paul's high standards of Christian living and church organization

Theme: How to "care for God's church" (3:5)

Contents:

1. Introduction (1)
   a. Salutation (1:1-2)
   b. Warning against heretics (1:3-11)
   c. Paul, formerly a sinner, now an apostle (1:12-17)
   d. Charge to Timothy (1:18-20)
2. Church life and organization (2:1-6:11)
   a. Directions for public worship (2)
   b. Qualifications of bishops and deacons (3)
   c. Warning against false teachers (4)
   d. How the pastor deals with his flock (5:1-6:11)
3. Final charge to Christians (6:12-10)

Introduction:

This letter together with 2 Timothy and Titus, all three of which deal with pastoral oversight in the Church, are referred to as the Pastoral Letters, or Pastoral Epistles. Though they appear to be letters, they are really pamphlets containing instruction for Church leaders. All three are similar in style and were undoubtedly written by the same author. They teach the same religious and ethical principles and share a common purpose: to show "how one ought to behave in the household of God, which is the church of the living God" (1 Tim 3:15).

These three letters were issued in Paul's name and addressed to his fellow workers, Timothy and Titus, but from their historical, theological, and ecclesiastical character, they appear to some scholars to have been written long after Paul's death. It is impossible to reconcile the facts of Paul's life as recorded in Acts and in his genuine letters with the general historical background of the Pastoral Letters. Furthermore, their theological outlook is not that of Paul. He preached that faith is supreme, but the Pastorals make loyalty to Church tradition paramount. Paul stressed inward fellowship with Christ, but the Pastorals emphasize the outward aspects of the Christian life. Paul mentioned the Holy Spirit more than eighty-three times in his letters, but the Pastorals only three times. In Paul's day, the Church had no official ministry, but by the time these letters were written there were bishops or elders, deacons, and probably an official staff of widows. The Pastorals, when read in their original Greek, are clearly different in vocabulary and style from Paul's authentic letters.

There are sections of the Pastorals, however, that appear to be brief personal notes from Paul. Among them are: 1 Tim 1:1-2; 2 Tim 1:1-11, 15-18; 2:1-13; 4:6-21; Titus 3:1-5,

The First Letter of Paul to Timothy

12-15. Possibly these are genuine fragments preserved by a disciple and later incorporated in the Pastorals.

In antiquity, writing under an assumed name was an accepted way of indicating the source from which an author drew his inspiration. In writing under Paul's name, therefore, the unknown author was not engaging in a fraud, but acknowledging his indebtedness to the great apostle. This writer, believing that Paul's doctrines and practical teachings embodied true Christianity, may have adapted them to the needs of his own day. From Paul's works he could have extracted rules governing Christian belief and practice that applied to a period of change when the Church was organizing itself, combatting pagan morals, and dealing with heresy.

Summaries of "sound doctrine" according to "the glorious gospel" of Paul and other apostles (1 Tim 1:10) are a feature of these letters (1 Tim 3:16; 2 Tim 1:8-10; 2:10-13; Titus 2:11-14; 3:5-7). Side by side with right belief, this author placed right action. He wrote about the personal character and behavior of church officials. He insisted on Christian ethical behavior, on courage, loyalty, uprightness, generosity, kindness, peace, purity of heart. Though in many beautiful and impressive passages he preached Christian living, he did not attain to Paul's deeper insight that right action is the "fruit" of the inward spiritual life. In placing Christian behavior and Christian faith in separate compartments, this writer anticipated much of the formalism of later Christianity.

He offered, however, a practical Christianity within the reach of all kinds of people. Ernest F. Scott in *The Moffatt New Testament Commentary* writes of this unknown man, that in his work

> the precepts of the Gospels, the aspirations of
> Paul and John, are transposed into a lower key.

But it may be truly said of this writer that while he compromises he does not abandon anything that is essential. He insists on the great Christian beliefs; he allows no debasing of the moral standards; he seeks to adapt the Church to existing conditions. . . . Because he has made Christianity a working religion for ordinary men, the author of the Pastorals may justly be ranked among the great Christian teachers.

* * * *

The most frequently misquoted verse in the Bible is probably 1 Timothy 6:10. This does *not* say that money is the root of evil but that "the *love* of money is the root of all evils." The writer goes on to characterize love of money as a "craving" that weakened the faith of some and "pierced their hearts with many pangs."

The Second Letter of Paul to Timothy

A Manual for Christian Leaders

Position: Sixteenth book of the New Testament

Date: About A.D. 100

Contents:

1. Salutation and thanksgiving (1:1-5)
2. Spiritual needs of a Christian teacher (1:6-2:13)
3. Counsels to a young minister (2:14-4:5)
   a. "Handling the word of truth" (2:14-19)

The Second Letter of Paul to Timothy

      b. "Correcting his opponents with gentleness" (2:20-26)
      c. Avoiding "men of corrupt mind and counterfeit faith" (3:1-9)
      d. Remembering Paul's example (3:10-13)
      e. Relying on the Scriptures (3:14-17)
      f. "Be steady, endure suffering, . . . fulfil your ministry" (4:1-5)
   4. Paul's farewell (4:6-22)
      a. His imminent death (4:6-8)
      b. His requests of Timothy (4:9-15)
      c. "The Lord . . . gave me strength to proclaim the word fully" (4:16-18)
   5. Greetings and benediction (4:19-22)

Introduction:

For the relation of this letter to the other Pastorals and for a discussion of its authorship, character, purpose, teachings, and value see the introduction to 1 Timothy.

* * * *

The only occurrence of the word *grandmother* in the Bible is in 2 Timothy 1:5 where Paul refers to Timothy's grandmother Lois. Innumerable grandfathers are mentioned in the Scriptures, but the word itself is now used in Exodus 10:6 in two recent English versions, the Revised Standard Version and the New American Bible.

* * * *

No more appropriate epitaph for the great apostle Paul could be written than the words, "I have fought the good fight, I have finished the race, I have kept the faith" (2 Tim 4:7).

The Letter of Paul to Titus

Counsels Concerning Doctrine and Good Works

Position: Seventeenth book of the New Testament
Date: About A.D. 100
Contents:

1. Salutation (1:1-4)
2. Qualifications for elders or bishops (1:5-16)
3. Themes for the Christian teacher (2:1-3:11)
4. Final instructions and greetings (3:12-15)

Introduction:

For the relation of this letter to 1 and 2 Timothy and for information about its author, its characteristics and purpose, and its value, see the introduction to 1 Timothy.

* * * *

For the first, or midnight Mass of Christmas, the Roman and the Sarum Missals and the *Book of Common Prayer* appoint Titus 2:11-15 to be read. These verses mention the first and the second "appearing" of Christ, both of which are for man's salvation and the gathering together of "a people of his own who are zealous for good deeds."

* * * *

This Letter, in enjoining bishops to be "hospitable" (1:8), evokes the difficulties and dangers encountered by 1st-century Christian missionaries on their travels. Overland journeys were usually by foot over perilous roads. When inns existed at all they offered wretched accommodations, consequently the safe haven and hospitality provided by Christian people was an important factor in spreading the gospel throughout the Mediterranean world (Acts 9:43; 21:16; Rom 16:2,23; 3 Jn 5-8; etc.).

The Letter of Paul to Philemon

A Plea for a Fugitive Slave

Position:	Eighteenth book of the New Testament
Date:	Between A.D. 53 and 58, during one of Paul's imprisonments
Author:	Paul
Style:	Eloquent, warmly personal
Written to:	Philemon, Apphia, Archippus, and the church in their house in Colossae, Asia Minor
Purpose:	To persuade the owner to forgive and take back his fugitive slave
Theme:	The brotherhood of Christ's followers

Contents:
1. Salutation (vv. 1-3)
2. Thanksgiving for Philemon's love and faith (vv. 4-7)
3. An appeal for Onesimus (vv. 8-20)
4. Conclusion and greeting (vv. 21-25)

Introduction:

This brief note, the only surviving personal letter written by Paul, is a tactful plea to a master on behalf of his slave. The apostle asked the master "for love's sake" to forgive his slave Onesimus, who had not only run away but had robbed him as well. While at large, the slave, after meeting Paul, had become a Christian. Though Paul found Onesimus helpful to him during his imprisonment and would have been glad to have him remain, he considered it his duty to send him back to his master—Philemon or possibly Archippus (Col 4:17).

In returning to his master, Onesimus exposed himself to danger. Fugitive slaves, according to the laws of the time, were subject to harsh punishment and often death. For the slave's safety, Paul not only gave him this letter but arranged for him to travel to his master's home in the company of Tychicus who was bearing another letter from Paul, this one addressed to the whole church in Colossae (Col 4:7-9).

Though the outcome of Onesimus' story is unknown, this letter would hardly have been preserved if Philemon had disregarded Paul's plea.

Why such a brief, personal note should have been considered worthy of being included among Paul's great letters is puzzling. Its appearance in Paul's collected writings might have been due to Onesimus' later prominence in the Church. There is a tradition that a certain Onesimus was bishop of Ephesus about A.D. 110. In that case a letter documenting his close relationship to the great apostle would have seemed important.

* * * *

Paul and the early Christians are sometimes criticized for not speaking out more vigorously against the widespread evil of slavery. Paul, however, attacked the spiritual roots of the evil. He labored to bring people into Christian fellowship as brothers and sisters in Christ. This new relationship in Christ is mentioned in his appeal to the slave owner to take back his runaway slave, "no longer as a slave but more than a slave, as a beloved brother . . . both in the flesh and in the Lord" (Philem 16).

The Letter to the Hebrews

A Treatise on the Significance of Christ

Position:	Ninteenth book of the New Testament
Date:	Between A.D. 75 and 100
Author:	Unknown
Style:	The best in the New Testament, formal, polished, eloquent, with a wide vocabulary
Addressed to:	A Christian community possibly with a Jewish background
Purpose:	To strengthen the faith of lukewarm Christians
Theme:	The excellence of Christ as mediator between God and man

Contents:

1. The superiority of Jesus Christ (1:1-3:6)
    a. To the prophets and angels (1-2)
    b. To Moses (3:1-6)
2. Warnings against unbelief (3:7-4:13)

3. Jesus the true high priest (4:14-5:10)
    a. Qualified by his human sympathy (4:14-5:3)
    b. Qualified by his divine appointment (5:4-10)
4. Exhortation to those who "have become dull of hearing" (5:11-6:12)
5. The completeness of Christ's sacrifice (6:13-10:18)
    a. The high priesthood of Christ "after the order of Melchizedek" (6:13-20)
    b. Comparison of Melchizedek and the Levitical priesthood (7)
    c. Christ's ministry "much more excellent than the old" (8)
    d. The effectiveness of his sacrifice (9:1-10:18)
6. Advice and warnings (10:19-39)
7. Hymn of faith (11)
8. Practical exhortations (12)
9. Concluding admonitions and blessing (13)

Introduction:

Because this great Christian document, referred to by its anonymous author as "my word of exhortation" (13:22), bears little resemblance to a letter except in its final verses, it may originally have been a sermon or a treatise. It was written to prove that Christianity is the fulfillment of Judaism and the supreme and absolute religion. At various places in the long and closely reasoned argument, the author inserted admonitions, warnings, encouragement, and advice to his readers.

The author's identity as well as that of his readers is unknown. Not until the end of the 2nd century was this document attributed to Paul. So different is it, however, in theology and literary style from Paul's letters that in A.D.

225 the Christian scholar Origen, though agreeing that Paul was responsible for its material, said that someone else—who he was "God only knows"—put the material in written form. Numerous possible authors have been considered including Barnabas, Luke, Apollos, Jude, Priscilla, and Clement of Rome. Some scholars suggest that the author was a Jewish Christian of Alexandria. His knowledge of the Scriptures, rabbinical logic, and literary style hint that he may have been a teacher of the Scriptures in that great Egyptian city. He wrote for other Jewish Christians who, either because of persecution or disappointment, were abandoning Christianity and returning to Judaism. The anonymous author aimed to inspire these Christians with pride in their religion, which, he declared, had at last brought them what all previous ages sought—an effective access to God.

Christianity, this writer believed, is the perfect religion. He showed that the prophets, angels, Moses, and the Jewish high priests were all mediators between God and man, but that Jesus, by virtue of his Sonship and because "He reflects the glory of God and bears the very stamp of his nature" (1:3), is greater than all of these mediators and is indeed the true high priest (8:1-2, 9:11-12). His earthly life and his sympathy with human suffering make him the final mediator between God and man. Instead of the daily sacrifice of the blood of animals, Christ as high priest poured out his own blood to accomplish man's forgiveness in a sacrifice never to be repeated.

The author of Hebrews based his argument on ritual ideas of the 1st century that have become strange and meaningless today. His argument and his many quotations from the Scriptures required a high degree of knowledge and intelligence on the part of his readers. His magnificent opening, however, is clear and unforgettable.

> In many and various ways God spoke of old
> to our fathers by the prophets; but in these
> last days he has spoken to us by a Son, whom
> he appointed the heir of all things, through whom
> also he created the world.
>
> Hebrews 1:1-2

Exhorting his readers to be loyal to their faith, this author defined faith as the power to perceive what is beyond our human senses. "Now faith is the assurance of things hoped for, the conviction of things not seen" (11:1). Faith enabled the glorious company of the heroes and heroines of old to achieve extraordinary things. But through Christ, who is "at the right hand of the Majesty on high" (1:3), we attain to a more lively faith. Christ has brought the unseen realities within our grasp.

> Therefore, since we are surrounded by so
> great a cloud of witnesses, let us also lay aside
> every weight, and sin which clings so closely,
> and let us run with perseverance the race that
> is set before us, looking to Jesus the pioneer
> and perfecter of our faith, who for the joy that
> was set before him endured the cross, despising
> the shame, and is seated at the right hand of
> the throne of God.
>
> Hebrews 12:1-2

* * * *

Renaissance artists, in portraying the Trinity, often showed Christ "seated at the right hand of the throne of God" (Heb 12:2). This imagery, which occurs four times in Hebrews (1:3; 8:1; 10:12), also appears in the Synoptic Gospels, Acts, and several of the letters.

* * * *

Instead of the customary purse of gold coins that courtiers usually gave to the English king on New Year's Day, Henry VIII received from Bishop Hugh Latimer a copy of the New Testament. In it the page containing Hebrews 13:4 was folded back so that the much-married Henry would not miss an implied rebuke that the bishop dared not utter, "Let marriage be held in honor among all. . . . "

The Letter of James

A Guide to Christian Living

Position: Twentieth book of the New Testament

Date: Between A.D. 75 and 100

Author: An unknown "James, a servant of God and the Lord Jesus Christ"

Style: Terse, forceful, imperative, epigrammatic

Written to: Members of the Church, the New Israel

Purpose: To recall Christians from worldliness and religious error to an understanding of the moral demands of their faith

Theme: "Be doers of the word, and not hearers only" (1:22)

Contents:

1. Salutation (1:1)
2. Patience in temptation (1:2-18)
3. True religion (1:19-27)

4. Impartiality and respect for all (2:1-13)
　　5. "Faith apart from works is barren" (2:14-26)
　　6. Bridling the tongue (3:1-12)
　　7. True and false wisdom (3:13-18)
　　8. Various counsels (4-5)
　　　a. Living in harmony (4:1-10)
　　　b. Slander and false confidence (4:11-17)
　　　c. The wickedness of the rich (5:1-6)
　　　d. The patience of the saints (5:7-12)
　　　e. The efficacy of prayer (5:13-18)
　　　f. The saving of sinners (5:19-20)

Introduction:

This document, which has been called "an ethical scrapbook," deals with the everyday aspects of Christianity and tells Christians how they ought to live. Though it mentions Christ only twice, it echoes his ethical teachings as expressed in the Sermon on the Mount. Its main emphasis is on Christian action rather than on the theological ideas and spiritual elements imparted by Paul and John. "Religion that is pure and undefiled before God and the Father is this: to visit orphans and widows in their affliction, and to keep oneself unstained from the world" (1:27).

In comparing the relative value of faith and works, the author declares that "faith apart from works is dead" (2:26), a statement that, on the surface, appears contrary to Paul's great doctrine of justification by faith alone. But, like this writer, Paul also believed in an active faith that issued in deeds (Rom 2:13). What this letter opposed was a heresy that distorted Paul's teaching and substituted hollow piety for active faith. To the writer, Christianity was much more than either a set of doctrines requiring mere intellectual acceptance or a series of self-contained devotional exercises. Christianity was a new way of life, a way that included: endurance (1:2-18); discipline (3:1-4:10), humility (4:11-5:6); patience (5:7-12); prayerfulness (5:13-18); and love (5:19-20).

As there is little evidence to support the tradition that the letter was written by "James the Lord's brother" (Gal 1:19), most scholars believe it is the work of a late 1st-century Christian teacher who wrote in an excellent Greek style. Though his document does not attain to great spiritual heights and fails to show that morality springs from a person's inward life in the spirit, it remains an important guide to Christian duties and right living.

* * * *

A mere "epistle of straw" and devoid of spiritual nourishment—such was Martin Luther's opinion of the letter. This great leader at the time of the Protestant Reformation objected to the assertion that "faith by itself, if it has no works, is dead" (Jas 2:17). Not so, protested Luther whose watchword was "justification by faith alone."

The First Letter of Peter

A Message of Christian Hope

Position: Twenty-first book of the New Testament

Date: Between A.D. 90 and 95

Author: Traditionally identified as Peter, but Silvanus (5:12) or another disciple of Peter may have been the actual author

Style: Rich vocabulary, skillful turns of phrase, excellent literary Greek

Written to: Christians of five northern provinces of Asia Minor

Purpose: To sustain Christians facing persecution

Theme: Christian hope and Christian living

Contents:

1. Salutation (1:1-2)
2. Christian hope (1:3-2:10)
   a. When facing persecution (1:3-12)
   b. Living worthy of this hope (1:13-2:10)
3. Christian conduct (2:11-4:6)
   a. Among unbelievers (2:11-12)
   b. In the state (2:13-17)
   c. In human relations (2:18-25)
   d. In the home (3:1-7)
   e. Under persecution (3:8-4:6)
4. Exhortations concerning personal Christianity (4:7-5:11)
5. Concluding remarks and greetings (5:12-14)

Introduction:

This letter, one of the finest and clearest examples of New Testament teaching, is filled with the spirit of Christian devotion. Martin Luther described it as one of the noblest letters of the New Testament. Some scholars regard its major section, 1:3-4:11, as a baptismal sermon. It was addressed to former pagans who faced hostility and even suffering because their Christian faith conflicted with emperor worship that was enforced by the state.

To encourage and sustain these new Christians in their coming trials, the author assured them that by sharing Christ's sufferings (4:13), they demonstrated the genuineness of their faith (1:7-11). He described Christianity as a "living hope through the resurrection of Jesus Christ from the dead" (1:3). Christ had redeemed them (1:18-19) and would support and reward them (2:25). The author exhorted them to live worthy of their Christian hope by submitting to the will of God and by leading blameless and peaceable lives. A feature of 1 Peter is its interweaving of faith and conduct, divine revelation and human action.

Though the salutation names the apostle Peter as the author, the letter is now often attributed to Silvanus (Silas) or an unknown Christian of Rome writing long after Peter's death. Arguments for and against Peter's authorship are many and complex. One of the most important involves the question—What persecution is mentioned in the letter? If Peter were the author, the persecution would necessarily have been the local one ordered by Nero in Rome, A.D. 64-65, when the apostle is believed to have suffered martyrdom. But the "fiery ordeal" (4:12) was obviously not confined to Rome, for here it apparently threatens not only the Christians in Asia Minor to whom this message is addressed (4:12-19), but the Christian "brotherhood throughout the world" (5:9). It was, then, probably the official, empire-wide persecution of Christians organized in A.D. 96 during Domitian's reign. If so, the letter itself must have been written at that time.

* * * *

A commonly misunderstood clause in the Apostles' Creed reads, "He descended into hell," meaning, "He went into the place of departed spirits." The belief that Christ visited the world of the dead between his death and resurrection was part of the earliest teaching of the Church (Mt 12:40; Acts 2:31) and is explicitly stated in 1 Peter 3:19 and 4:6. These verses are variously interpreted. Some see in them a belief that Christ visited Hades, the world of the dead, to win his final victory over Satan; others, that he went to preach his gospel to those who had died before his coming so that they, too, might attain eternal life in him.

* * * *

James I of England had the last word in the defense of his mother, Mary Queen of Scots, who had been executed by Queen Elizabeth for treason. On the canopy above her tomb in Westminster Abbey the king cited 1 Peter 2:22. This reads, "committed no sin; no guile was found on his lips."

The Second Letter of Peter

The Last-Written Book of the New Testament

Position: Twenty-second book of the New Testament

Date: About A.D. 150

Author: Unknown

Style: Impersonal, erudite, with clumsy sentences

Written to: Christians in general

Purposes: To warn against heretical teachers and to restore belief in the second coming of Christ

The Second Letter of Peter

Theme: Knowledge of Christ as the source of "grace and peace . . . [and of] all things that pertain to life and godliness" (1:2-3)

Contents:

1. Salutation (1:1-2)
2. Exhortation to grow in knowledge and grace (1:3-11)
3. Assurance of Christian salvation (1:12-21)
4. Denunciation of heretical teachers (2)
5. Certainty of Christ's second coming (3:1-13)
6. The duty of Christians (3:14-18)

Introduction:

This document, though written in the form of a letter, is actually a religious discourse or homily exhorting Christians to stand fast in the faith, to avoid false teachers, and to maintain their faith in the return of Christ. Possibly because this work is not among the great New Testament writings, it was for many years excluded from the canon. Nevertheless, its information about the trials and uncertainties of the hardpressed, 2nd-century Church gives it historical importance.

A 2nd-century date for 2 Peter is supported by the evidence that many Christians, having abandoned hope of the second coming of Christ, were asking, "Where is the promise of his coming? For ever since the fathers fell asleep, all things have continued as they were from the beginning of creation" (3:4). Moreover, its author knew many of the New Testament documents. He comments that Paul's letters were being misinterpreted by ignorant people to advance their own views (3:15-16). He knew 1 Peter, for he said of his own work, "This is now the second letter that I have written to you" (3:1). He indicated that Peter's recollections were the basis for Mark's Gospel (1:15). He was familiar with the account of the transfiguration in the Synoptic Gospels (1:17-18), and the prediction of Peter's martyrdom as reported in the appendix to John's Gospel (1:14 cf. Jn 21:18-19). Finally, he incorporated in his own work verses 4-18 of the Letter of Jude.

The author's knowledge of all these New Testament writings makes it unlikely that he could have been the apostle Peter, for it is probable that Peter died in Nero's persecutions of A.D. 64-65. The use of Peter's name, however, was at that time a common literary fiction to remind the Church of the apostolic source of the letter's teachings. Its fictitious authorship is similar to that of such apocryphal works as the *Gospel of Peter* and the *Apocalypse of Peter*, which were also attributed to Peter.

2 Peter, the last New Testament document to be written, ends on a note of hope, "We wait for a new heaven and a new earth in which righteousness dwells" (3:13).

* * * *

A clue to the origin of the New Testament occurs in 2 Peter 3:15-16 where the author mentions Paul's letters as a collection that is being widely read. In the same sentence this author speaks of "the *other* scriptures," meaning the Old Testament Scriptures, which comprised the Bible of the earliest Christians. At this early date, according to this letter, Paul's collected teachings were being read and treasured as an authoritative body of Christian writings worthy to stand beside the Old Testament Scriptures.

The First Letter of John

A Letter Explaining True Christianity

Position:	Twenty-third book of the New Testament
Date:	About A.D. 100
Author:	Unknown, but traditionally thought to be the same person who wrote the Gospel of John
Style:	Spontaneous, simple, with striking aphorisms
Written to:	Members of the churches under the care of the author
Purposes:	To deepen the spiritual life of church members and to combat heresy
Theme:	"And this is his commandment, that we should believe in the name of his Son Jesus Christ and love one another" (3:23)

Contents:

1. Introduction (1:1-4)
2. True Christianity contrasted with false doctrine (1:5-2:29)
3. Living in the family of God (3)
4. Tests of faith (4:1-5:3)
   a. The test of belief (4:1-6)
   b. The test of brotherly love (4:7-21)
   c. The test of obedience to God (5:1-3)
5. Assurance of victory (5:4-12)
6. Conclusion: repetition of the themes of the letter (5:13-21)

Introduction:

This outstanding statement of Christian truth, though it lacks the salutation and concluding greetings of the usual Greek letter, was probably not a tract or sermon but a circular letter written to remind a particular group of Christians of the fundamentals of their faith. These people may have been members of several churches in the neighborhood of Ephesus where the letter probably originated. The author was doubtless their revered leader, for he addressed them affectionately as "my little children" (2:1) or "beloved" (4:1).

The identity of this author is not known. It is possible that he was the author of the Gospel of John, for both documents are similar in vocabulary, style, and ideas. There is no certainty, however, that he was the apostle John, or a certain Elder John of Ephesus, as some people have tried to prove.

At the time this letter was written, a distorted form of Christianity, probably an early type of Gnosticism, was being preached by "false prophets" (4:1-6) who, believing that matter is inherently evil, denied that Christ had "come in the flesh" (4:2). Against this error, the author of 1 John again and again declared that the historic Jesus is the Christ (4:2; 5:1,20). The heretics laid claim to spirituality and mystical experience, boasting, "We have no sin" and "I know him" (1:8; 2:4). But the author said that these people neglected Christian morality and Christian love.

Instead of trying to refute false ideas, the author applied basic Christian teaching to the needs of his readers. The great themes of Christian theology and Christian living are all presented, not in a formal, logical way, but blended together in different combinations like recurring melodies in music. Though the sentences are simple, the truth they convey is profound.

The author emphasized that believers already know God, have fellowship with the Father and Son, and possess eternal life (5:12-13). To know God, he said, is to obey his commandments, for real religion includes ethical living (2:4-6). He taught that eternal life is characterized by love and is lived in fellowship (1:3). His unique contribution to Christian theology is his profound yet simple summary of the Christian revelation of God, "God is love" (4:8,16).

* * * *

Helen Keller lived all but the first two of her eighty-eight years in the silent darkness of complete blindness and deafness. When Helen was a child, her teacher, Anne Sullivan Macy, succeeded in penetrating her black and soundless world and in communicating with her, eventually teaching her to understand signs, to speak, and to "read" Braille. After graduating with honors from Radcliffe, Helen Keller wrote books, lectured, and traveled widely. Her favorite Bible verse was from this letter, "God is light and in him is no darkness at all" (1 Jn 1:5).

The Second Letter of John

A Personal Letter to a Local Church

Position: Twenty-fourth book of the New Testament

Date: Between A.D. 100 and 110

Author: "The Elder," who is identified by some scholars as the author of 1 and 3 John as well as the Gospel of John

Written to:	Members of a local church visited by the author
Purpose:	To warn against false teachers
Theme:	Love and truth

Introduction:

The Elder addressed this brief letter to "the Lady chosen by God, and her children" (NEB) undoubtedly referring, not to a Christian matron and her family, but to a local church over which he exercised authority. He warned the members not to extend hospitality to certain false teachers who were planning to visit them. Echoing 1 John, the Elder insisted that love of others and faith in Christ are the simple, everlasting truths of the Christian message.

The Third Letter of John

A Private Note Concerning a Church Dispute

Position:	Twenty-fifth book of the New Testament
Date:	Between A.D. 100 and 110
Author:	"The Elder"
Style:	Similar to that of 1 and 2 John
Written to:	Gaius
Purpose:	To gain Gaius' help and support during the Elder's forthcoming visit
Theme:	The Elder's dispute with Diotrephes

Introduction:

Four men were involved in this dispute:
- The Elder, who sent the letter;
- Demetrius, the Elder's emissary, who delivered it;
- Gaius, a loyal friend of the Elder as well as an influential layman in a local church and the recipient of the letter;
- Diotrephes, a local church leader who had challenged the authority of the Elder.

The Elder describes Diotrephes as a man who "likes to put himself first and does not acknowledge my authority." Diotrephes had refused to receive emissaries from the Elder and had even excommunicated church members who gave them hospitality—an indication that serious disagreements began early in the life of the Church. Did this conflict spring from the arrogance of youth versus the paternalism of an old missionary, or did it involve some real question of doctrine? Though this question is unanswerable, the portrait of Gaius in this letter bears the unmistakable imprint of a true Christian.

The Letter of Jude

A Tract Against Heresy

Position:	Twenty-sixth book of the New Testament
Date:	Between A.D. 100 and 120
Author:	Unknown, though traditionally identified as the brother of James and of Jesus (Mk 6:3)
Style:	Vigorous, eloquent, picturesque

Written for: All Christians, though the author probably had a particular church or group of churches in mind

Purposes: To oppose heresy and affirm the trustworthiness of the apostolic faith

Theme: The struggle of Christianity against heresy

Contents:

1. Salutation (vv. 1-2)
2. Reasons for writing (vv. 3-4)
3. Denunciation of heretics (vv. 5-19)
4. Exhortation to stand fast in the faith (vv. 20-23)
5. Doxology (vv. 24-25)

Introduction:

Jude combatted a heresy, probably an early form of Gnosticism, that threatened the life of the Church. The heretics, whom he described as immoral (vv. 7,16), were "ungodly persons who pervert the grace of our God into licentiousness and deny our only Master and Lord, Jesus Christ" (v. 4). They were further characterized as covetous (vv. 11,16), rebellious against authority (vv. 8,11), "grumblers, malcontents . . . loud-mouthed boasters" (v. 16) who, even at the sacred meals, "boldly carouse together" (v. 12). They boasted about their own spirituality, which they thought sufficient to excuse them from the ordinary rules of decent behavior. They flouted the usual moral laws, claiming that anything they chose to do was right. As a result, they indulged in many kinds of sensuality, thus making themselves a scandal in the Church. Jude lashed out against these people calling them clouds without rain, trees without fruit, raging waves and "wandering [shooting] stars for whom the nether gloom of darkness has been reserved for ever" (v. 13).

The traditions identifying this author with one of the Twelve (Lk 6:16) or with Judas the brother of James of Jerusalem and of Jesus (Mk 6:3) are not convincing in view of the fact that the writer of this letter does not claim to be an apostle (v. 17). Furthermore, in exhorting his readers "to contend for the faith which was once for all delivered to the saints" (v. 3), he seems to be looking back to the apostolic age and implying that Christianity was established long ago.

* * * *

In the Bible, ascriptions of praise and glory to God range from *hallelujah*, "praise ye the Lord," to the elaborate and beautiful doxology with which this otherwise pedestrian letter ends. The doxology, touching upon both judgment and salvation, is sometimes used today as a benediction.

The Revelation to John

The New Testament Apocalypse

Position: Twenty-seventh and last book of the New Testament

Date: About A.D. 95

Author: A certain John of unknown identity

Style: Descriptive splendor, superb poetic imagery, but expressed in inferior Greek

Written for: The Christians of Asia Minor

Purpose: To inspire faith and courage in Christians facing persecution

Theme: "The Lord our God the Almighty reigns" (19:6)

Contents:
1. Prologue (1:1-3)
2. Letters to the seven churches of Asia (1:4-3:22)
    a. Salutation and first vision (1:4-20)
    b. To Ephesus (2:1-7)
    c. To Smyrna (2:8-11)
    d. To Pergamum (2:12-17)
    e. To Thyatira (2:18-29)
    f. To Sardis (3:1-6)
    g. To Philadelphia (3:7-13)
    h. To Laodicea (3:14-22)
3. Visions (4:1-22:5)
    a. The glory of God and of the Lamb (4-5)
    b. Opening of the seven seals (6:1-8:5)
    c. Seven angels with trumpets and seven woes (8:6-11:19)
    d. Seven oracles of the last days (12-14)
    e. Seven last plagues (15-16)
    f. The fall of "Babylon" (17:1-19:10)
    g. Final victory and judgment (19:11-20:15)
    h. A "new heaven and a new earth" (21:1-22:5)
4. Epilogue (22:6-21)

The Revelation to John

Introduction:

The author of this strange book called himself John, a servant of Jesus and brother and companion in tribulation of the Christians of Asia Minor (1:1, 4, 9). His tribulation was apparently his imprisonment and forced labor in the stone quarries of Patmos, an island off the coast of Asia Minor near Ephesus (1:9-10). There he experienced extraordinary visions. Though this John did not claim apostolic authority or personal knowledge of the historical Jesus, the possibility that he was the apostle John cannot be ruled out entirely. He is often called John the Divine, meaning John the Theologian. Because of the differences in style and subject matter between Revelation on the one hand and the Gospel and Letters of John on the other, it is difficult to support the theory that the author of Revelation wrote any of the other works. His identity remains an open question.

Revelation is filled with symbolic visions and haunting images of things to come, all of which are characteristic of the type of Hebrew and Christian literature that developed from prophecy and was called apocalypse. Apocalypses were common in Judaism during the despair of the Hellenistic period and outstanding examples occur in the books of Ezekiel and Daniel. On occasion, Jesus used language and modes of thought derived from the popular apocalyptic writing of his day (Mk 13).

John believed that the crisis facing the Church in the reign of Domitian, when Christians encountered their first serious persecution, was the prelude to God's intervention in human affairs. He wrote to prepare his readers for the coming of Satan and supernatural terrors. According to the apocalypses, these terrors were to be the final events before the end of the existing world order and the beginning of the new age. In recording his extravagant and bizarre vision, John wrote of dire events that cannot be taken literally and are virtually incomprehensible except to those acquainted with apocalyptic literature.

Historically, John's apocalyptic prophecies were not fulfilled. Domitian was succeeded by the five good emperors, not by Satan. Rome did not fall, but continued to rule for several centuries. The world did not end, nor did Christ return to judge humanity. The failure of John's predictions induced later readers to search for fulfillment in their own times, but it is evident that his visions were recorded for his own contemporaries, not for the remote future. He wrote of "what must soon take place . . . for the time is near" (1:1,3; 22:10). He believed that Christ's return was imminent: "Behold, I am coming soon" (22:12).

This strange book paints unforgettable pictures that have stirred the imaginations of poets and other creative artists. Philip Carrington, a former Archbishop of Quebec and a scholar, views it as "a work of genius of the same order as the *Divine Comedy* of Dante or the *Paradise Lost* of Milton." It is indeed, as Donald Coggan, Archbishop of Canterbury, 1974-1980 writes, the "most grim book of the New Testament . . . [yet it] is shot through with songs of triumph." From the author's frightening apocalyptic images emerges his courageous faith that God reigns, that those who trust in him and obey him need not fear anything, and that victory for Christ and his Church is assured. At the sound of a trumpet the angels sing, "The kingdom of the world has become the kingdom of our Lord and of his Christ, and he shall reign for ever and ever" (11:15).

With a burst of exultation, Revelation brings the Bible to an end in a final vision of humankind and all creation transformed by the glory of God.

> Then I saw a new heaven and a new earth;
> for the first heaven and the first earth had

The Revelation to John

passed away. . . . And I saw the holy city, new
Jerusalem, coming down out of heaven from God,
prepared as a bride adorned for her husband;
and I heard a great voice from the throne
saying, "Behold, the dwelling of God is with
men. He will dwell with them, and they shall
be his people . . . he will wipe every tear from
their eyes, and death shall be no more, neither
shall there be mourning nor crying nor pain
any more, for the former things, have passed
away."

Revelation 21:1-4

* * * *

Among the ten largest cities of the United States, the only one having the name of a Biblical city is Philadelphia. In Greek this means "brotherly love." One of the seven churches of Asia to whom John wrote was located at Philadelphia, southeast of Sardis. The city, founded in the middle of the 2nd century B.C. by Attalus II Philadelphus, one of Alexander's heirs, was destroyed by an earthquake in A.D. 17. Its rebuilding by Emperor Tiberius (Lk 3:1) is possibly alluded to in the reference to building in Revelation 3:12. Alashehir is the modern town on the site of ancient Philadelphia.

* * * *

The Four Horsemen of the Apocalypse (Rev 6:1-8) comprise perhaps the most famous allegorical group in the Bible, though what these visionary figures represent is not entirely clear. The rider on the white horse may signify Christ; the figure on the red horse, war; on the black horse, the famine that follows war; and the last rider on the pale horse, pestilence and death that result from famine.

* * * *

The primary theme of the Bible is the special relation of the people of God to their Lord, but another theme, like a counterpoint, is heard with increasing urgency in the prophets and the New Testament. This theme is the oneness of all humankind before God. Finally, in Revelation a doxology is sung to Christ who

> " . . . didst ransom men for God
> from every tribe and tongue and people
> and nation,
> and has made them a kingdom and priests
> to our God,
> and they shall reign on earth."
>
> Revelation 5:9-10

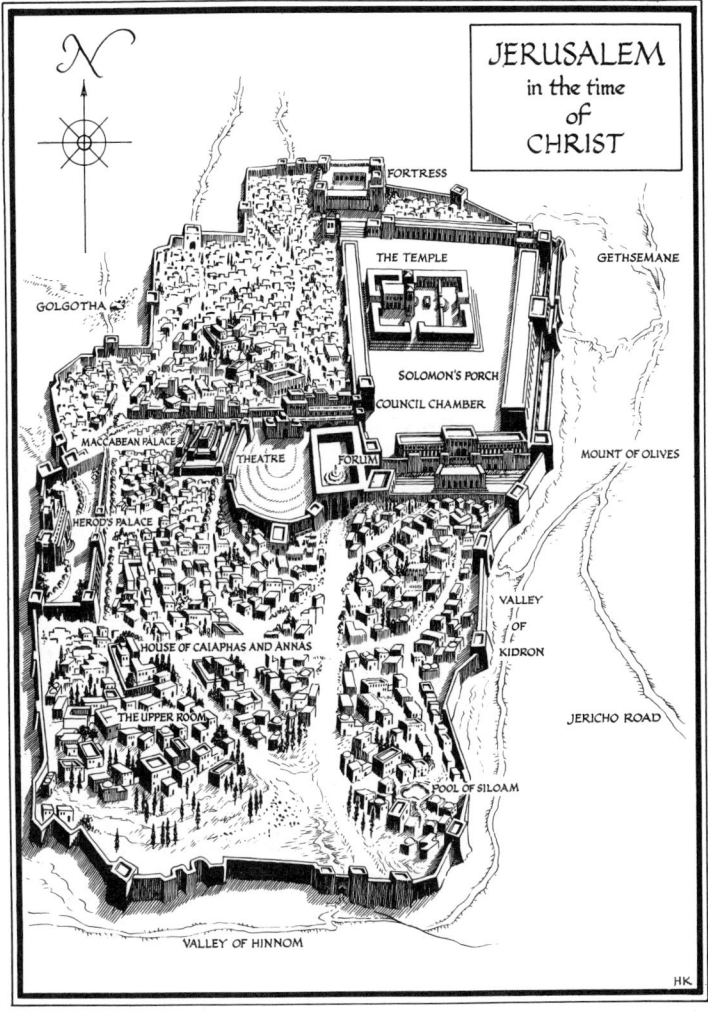

Horace Knowles   British & Foreign Bible Society, London.

The Deeds and Words of Jesus Christ

A Harmony of the Gospels

This table of references is designed to show the comparable or parallel accounts in the four Gospels and to provide readers with a synopsis of the Biblical records concerning Jesus.

Because the Gospels seldom include precise notes of time and place when they report the various incidents of Jesus' ministry and because the order of events sometimes differs from one Gospel to another, it is virtually impossible to reconstruct the original chronological sequence of Jesus' life or to trace with certainty his movements from place to place. Even the length of his ministry remains a question. Mark apparently implies that it lasted a year, or perhaps two, while John records three Passovers one of which was attended by Jesus in Jerusalem.

Despite these uncertainties, it is generally agreed that Mark, which is probably the earliest Gospel and the one on which Matthew and Luke seem to be based, presents a reliable summary of what Jesus said and did. For this reason the following synopsis or harmony of the Gospels follows the sequence of events reported in Mark. Additional material from the other Gospels is placed in Mark's general framework. For a more detailed analysis of the Gospel material, see *Gospel Parallels: A Synopsis of the First Three Gospels*, New York: Thomas Nelson & Sons, 1949.

The items below that are starred (*) record the miracles of Jesus.

	Matthew	Mark	Luke	John
Prologue				
Introduction			1:1-4	
"The Word became flesh"				1:1-18
Genealogies	1:1-17		3:23-38	
Angels foretell Jesus' birth	1:18-25		1:26-38	
John the Baptist's birth is foretold			1:5-25	
Mary visits her kinswoman Elizabeth			1:39-56	
John is born to Zechariah and Elizabeth			1:57-80	
Jesus' Birth and Infancy				
Jesus is born	2:1		2:1-20	
Wise Men honor him	2:1-12			
He is named and later presented in the Temple			2:21-38	
His parents flee with him to Egypt	2:13-18			
He spends his childhood in Nazareth	2:19-23		2:39-40	
Preparation for His Mission				
Jesus visits Jerusalem as a boy			2:41-52	
John the Baptist preaches to multitudes	3:1-12	1:1-8	3:1-20	
Jesus is baptized by John	3:13-17	1:9-11	3:21-22	
Jesus wrestles with spiritual temptation	4:1-11	1:12-13	4:1-13	
The Early Ministry of Jesus According to John's Gospel				
Jesus calls his first disciples				1:19-28
				1:29-34
				1:35-51
*Attends a wedding feast				2:1-12

113

	Matthew	Mark	Luke	John
Visits Jerusalem at the Passover				2:13-25
Receives Nicodemus at night				3:1-21
Begins a ministry of baptism in Judea				3:22-24
Departs for Galilee				4:1-3
Converses with a woman in Samaria				4:4-42
*Heals an official's son				4:43-54
*Heals a lame man at the pool				5:1-18
Discourses about the Son and the Father				5:19-47
His Great Ministry in Galilee				
Announces the arrival of the Kingdom of God	4:12-17	1:14-15	4:14-15	
*Calls four disciples	4:18-22	1:16-20	5:1-11	1:35-42
Teaches in the synagogue at Capernaum	7:28-29	1:21-22	4:31-32	
*Exorcises an unclean spirit		1:23-28	4:33-37	
*Cures Peter's mother-in-law and many others	8:14-17	1:29-34	4:38-41	
Sets forth on a preaching tour	4:23-25; 9:35-38	1:35-39	4:42-44	
*Cleanses a leper	8:1-4	1:40-45	5:12-16	
*Heals the centurion's servant	8:5-13		7:1-10	
*Forgives and heals a paralytic	9:1-8	2:1-12	5:17-26	
Calls Matthew (Levi) to discipleship	9:9-13	2:13-17	5:27-32	
Answers a question about fasting	9:14-17	2:18-22	5:33-39	
*Disputes with the Pharisees and heals a man with a withered hand	12:1-14	2:23-3:6	6:1-11	
*Performs "mighty works" of healing	4:23-24; 12:15-21; 15:29-31	3:7-12	6:17-19	

Chooses and instructs twelve disciples	10:1-5	3:13-19	6:12-16
*Heals a demoniac and replies to the Pharisees	12:22-37	3:20-30	11:14-23
Explains the actions of unclean spirits	12:43-45		11:24-26
Blesses those who hear and keep the word of God			11:27-28
Teaches the parable of the lighted lamp	5:14-16	4:21	11:33-36
Asks, "Who are my mother and my brothers?"	12:46-50	3:31-35	8:19-21
Teaches the parable of the sower	13:1-52	4:1-34	8:4-18
Replies to would-be disciples	8:18-22		9:57-62
*Calms a storm at sea	8:23-27	4:35-41	8:22-25
*Exorcises the Gerasene demoniac	8:28-34	5:1-20	8:26-39
*Raises Jairus' daughter and cures a woman who touches his garment	9:18-26	5:21-43	8:40-56
*Restores sight to two blind men and heals a dumb demoniac	9:27-34		
Encounters unbelief at Nazareth	13:53-58	6:1-6	4:16-30
Sends forth twelve disciples	10:1,5-42	6:7-13	9:1-6
Collections of the Teachings of Jesus			
The Sermon on the Mount	5:1-7:29		
The Sermon on the Plain			6:17-49
A group of parables and teachings			12:13-18:14
Jesus and John the Baptist				
John endorses Jesus				3:25-36
John seeks to know who Jesus is	11:1-6		7:18-23
Jesus explains his relation to John	11:7-19		7:24-35

	Matthew	Mark	Luke	John
John's imprisonment and death	14:1-12	6:14-29	3:19-20; 9:7-9	
The Continuing Ministry of Jesus				
Receives the report of his disciples	14:13-14	6:30-33	9:10-11	
*Feeds five thousand people	14:15-21	6:34-44	9:12-17	6:1-14
*Walks on the water	14:22-33	6:45-52		6:15-21
Teaches that he is "the bread of life"				6:22-65
Is deserted by all but the Twelve				6:66-71
*Restores health to many at Gennesaret	14:34-36	6:53-56		
Argues with the Pharisees about ritual	15:1-20	7:1-23		
Gives thanks in prayer	11:25-27		10:21-22	
Comforts the heavy laden	11:28-30			
*Raises a widow's son at Nain			7:11-17	
Dines at a Pharisee's house where a sinful woman anoints him			7:36-50	
Departs on a preaching tour			8:1-3	
*Cures the daughter of a Gentile woman	15:21-28	7:24-30		
*Restores hearing and speech to a deaf mute		7:31-37		
*Feeds four thousand people	15:32-39	8:1-10		
Declines to give the Pharisees a "sign from heaven"	12:38-42; 16:1-4	8:11-13	11:29-32	
Warns against the Pharisees	16:5-12	8:14-21	12:1	
*Heals a blind man at Bethsaida		8:22-26		
Questions the disciples, "Who do you say that I am?"	16:13-23	8:27-33	9:18-22	6:66-71

Teaches the meaning of discipleship	16:24-28	8:34-9:1	9:23-27
Is transfigured on the mountain	17:1-13	9:2-13	9:28-36
*Cures an epileptic boy	17:14-21	9:14-29	9:37-43
Predicts his death and resurrection	17:22-23	9:30-32	9:43-45
*Pays the Temple tax with coin from fish's mouth	17:24-27		
Sets a child before the disciples as an example	18:1-5	9:33-37	9:46-48
Teaches about temptation, forgiveness, and other matters	18:6-35	9:42-50	17:1-10
Comments on the unknown exorcist		9:38-41	9:49-50
Attends the Feast of Tabernacles in Jerusalem				7:1-53
Answers those who condemn the adulteress				8:1-11
Teaches that he is "the light of the world"				8:12-59
*Gives sight to a man born blind				9:1-41
Incidents on His Last Journey toward Jerusalem				
Departs from Galilee	19:1-2	10:1	9:51
Encounters opposition in Samaria			9:52-56
Sends forth seventy disciples	9:37-38		10:1-12
Pronounces woe on the cities of Galilee	11:20-24		10:13-16
Welcomes the return of the seventy			10:17-24
Teaches the parable of the Good Samaritan			10:29-37
Visits the home of Martha and Mary			10:38-42
Teaches his disciples to pray	6:5-15		11:1-13
Warns against Pharisaism	23:1-36		11:37-54
Encourages his disciples			12:1-13:9

	Matthew	Mark	Luke	John
*Frees a woman from her infirmity			13:10-17	
Speaks about the "first who will be last"	7:13-14; 8:11-12		13:22-30	
Carries on his works of mercy despite Herod's threat			13:31-33	
Laments over Jerusalem	23:37-39		13:34-35	
*Dines with a Pharisee and cures a man suffering from dropsy			14:1-24	
Explains the conditions of discipleship			14:25-35	
Teaches four parables: the Lost Sheep, the Coin, the Prodigal Son, the Dishonest Steward			15:1-16:13	
Replies to the scoffing Pharisees			16:14-17	
Tells the story of the Rich Man and Lazarus			16:19-31	
*Cleanses ten lepers			17:11-19	
Announces, "the kingdom of God is in the midst of you"			17:20-21	
Deals with the question of divorce	19:3-12	10:2-12	16:18	
Tells two parables			18:1-14	
Welcomes little children	19:13-15	10:13-16	18:15-17	
Counsels a rich young ruler	19:16-30	10:17-31	18:18-30	
Teaches the parable of the Vineyard Laborers	20:1-16			
Warns his disciples of his coming death	20:17-19	10:32-34	18:31-34	
Proclaims, "I am the good shepherd"				10:1-21
Attends the Feast of Dedication in Jerusalem				10:22-39

Crosses the Jordan into Perea	19:1-2		10:40-42
*Raises Lazarus to Life			11:1-45
Leaves Jerusalem because of a plot against his life			11:46-57
Replies to the request of James and John	20:20-28	10:35-45	22:24-27
*Restores sight to Bartimaeus and others at Jericho	20:29-34	10:46-52	18:35-43
Dines with Zacchaeus			19:1-10
His Final Days in Jerusalem			
Enters the city in triumph	21:1-11	11:1-11	19:28-44	12:12-16
*Curses the barren fig tree	21:18-22	11:12-14, 20-26		
Cleanses the Temple	21:12-13	11:15-17	19:45-46	2:13-25
Wins popular acclaim	21:14-17	11:18-19	19:47-48	12:17-19
Is sought after by certain Greeks				12:20-23
Declines to answer a question about his authority	21:23-27	11:27-33	20:1-8	
Narrates parables of the Two Sons, the Wicked Tenants, the Marriage Feast	21:28; 22:14	12:1-12	20:9-19	
Avoids entrapment on questions of taxes and of the resurrection	22:15-33	12:13-27	20:20-40	
Answers a question about the greatest commandment	22:34-40	12:28-34	10:25-28	
Asks, "What do you think of the Christ?"	22:41-46	12:35-37	20:41-44	
Inveighs against the scribes and Pharisees	23:1-36	12:38-40	20:45-47	

	Matthew	Mark	Luke	John
Observes a poor widow make her offering		12:41-44	21:1-4	
Predicts the end of the age	24:1-51	13:1-37	17:22-37; 21:5-36	
A summary of the days in Jerusalem			21:37-38	
Tells the parable of the Wise and Foolish Maidens, the Talents (pounds), and the Great Judgment	25:1-46		19:11-27	
Dines in Bethany and is anointed	26:6-13	14:3-9		12:1-11
Ends his public ministry				12:24-50
The Narrative of His Death				
The chief priests hire Judas to betray Jesus	26:1-5, 14-16	14:1-2, 10-11	22:1-6	
Jesus prepares for the Passover	26:17-19	14:12-16	22:7-13	
He sits at table with his disciples	26:20-25	14:17-21	22:14,21-30	13:1-38
He institutes the Lord's Supper	26:26-29	14:22-25	22:15-20	
He foretells his betrayal and Peter's denial	26:30-35	14:26-31	22:21-23, 31-38	
He discourses on many subjects				14:1-16:33
He prays to his Father				17:1-26
He goes to Gethsemane	26:36-46	14:32-42	22:39-46	18:1
Judas betrays him	26:47-56	14:43-53	22:47-48	18:2-12
*Jesus heals the servant's ear			22:49-52	
The Sanhedrin tries him; Peter denies him	26:57-27:2	14:53-15:1	22:54-71	18:13-27
Pilate sentences him to death	27:11-31	15:2-20	23:1-25	18:28-19:16

120

Jesus bears his cross to Golgotha	27:32-33	15:21-22		19:17
He is crucified and dies	27:33-56	15:23-41		19:18-37
His friends place his body in the tomb	27:57-61	15:42-47		19:38-42
Pilate sets a guard at his tomb	27:62-66; 28:11-15			
Judas repents and dies	27:3-10			
The Resurrection				
The women find his tomb empty	28:1-8	16:1-8	24:1-12	20:1-10
Mary Magdalene and the women meet the risen Christ	28:9-10	(16:9-11)†		20:11-18
Christ encounters two disciples on the Emmaus road		(16:12-13)†	24:13-35	
He appears to the disciples in Jerusalem			24:36-49	20:19-23
He commissions his disciples to go into the whole world	28:16-20	(16:14-18)†		
Thomas and the other disciples see the risen Christ				20:24-31
*Seven disciples meet Christ in Galilee; the great catch of fish				21:1-25
Christ blesses his disciples and takes leave of them		(16:19)†	24:50-53	

† From the longer ending of Mark

The Parables of Jesus

The most characteristic literary form used by Jesus was the parable. These imaginary anecdotes are effective in teaching because they link whatever is to be learned with something that is already familiar. In the Old Testament there are a few true parables, notably Nathan's story of the ewe lamb (2 Sam 12:1-7) and Isaiah's song of the vineyard (Isa 5:1-7). Parables, however, are uniquely associated with Jesus.

Parables are dramatic stories that teach, not by direct assertion, but indirectly and subtly by comparison or analogy. They picture life as it is, and with their very human characters, their homely details, and their swiftly moving plots, they immediately capture our attention. Though we first notice the story itself, we next ask ourselves, "What is the point of this story?" As one of the characters in a P.G. Wodehouse story observed, a parable sounds at first like a simple tale, but it "keeps something up its sleeve which suddenly pops up and leaves you flat." A good example of this is the parable of the Good Samaritan.

Jesus told these compact little stories to his disciples, to the crowds, to individual questioners, and to the scribes and Pharisees who were often in the background, sometimes objecting and heckling. Master teacher that he was, "he taught them many things in parables" (Mk 4:2) in order to lead his hearers from the known and familiar to the unknown and hitherto unimaginable. In this way he encouraged people to think and to discover the truth for themselves. It was never his way to compel agreement or to force his message on the unthinking or the unwilling. His parables quickened the imagination and provided challenges to thought and decision. The responsibility for accepting or rejecting him and his message he left with each man or woman.

Surely, Jesus did not clothe his message in parables in order to conceal it from the crowds, as Mark 4:11-12 seems to suggest. Instead, we observe him telling these powerful little stories to help even simple, uneducated people understand and remember his message. Inevitably, some saw, but did not perceive—they heard, but did not heed. Matthew explains this disappointing outcome in words from Isaiah.

> For this people's heart has grown dull,
> and their ears are heavy of hearing,
> and their eyes have closed.
>
> Matthew 13:15

Many, however, of the common people of Galilee and Judea hung upon his words, for he taught graciously and powerfully. He spoke, so the people reported, "with authority" and they "heard him gladly." Well they might, for in the judgment of the poet Tennyson, his parables are "perfection beyond compare."

The parables reveal much about Jesus himself—his extraordinary originality, his quick understanding, his ability to create apt images, his gift for poetry, his keen interest in human beings and their predicaments, and his hearty enjoyment of the color, movement, and events of the real world. These stories demonstrate how well he understood the daily struggles and joys of ordinary living. In the parables we see his mind at work, bearing down swiftly on the heart of each issue, avoiding cloudy abstractions, and expressing his message naturally and simply in concrete pictures.

Besides putting us in touch with Jesus himself, his parables afford a lively picture of life in first-century Palestine.

They document the concerns of such people as its farmers and shepherds, its vineyard laborers and rich men, its careless young sons, its unjust judges, its poor housewives for whom a lost coin is a calamity.

The chief value of the parables, however, is not their literary charm, their historical authenticity, or even the insight they afford into the personality of Jesus. Their importance lies in the fact that they convey the central message of his ministry. The clues to interpreting the parables are not moral and religious principles. The parables are not dramatized proverbs. They are not leisurely teachings about good ways to conduct one's individual life. Rather the clue to an understanding of the parables is the crucial moment in history when they were spoken. This is expressed in Jesus' first proclamation: "The time is fulfilled, and the kingdom of God is at hand; repent, and believe the gospel" (Mk 1:15). The coming of Jesus inaugurated the reign of God. This was the present reality to which he called men and women. "Behold, the kingdom of God is in the midst of you" (Lk 17:20). The future consummation of that kingdom is expressed in his prayer, "Thy kingdom come." The key to the parables is the kingdom that is both present and to come. It is here and now in Christ until it finally dawns in its fulness.

In brief, the parables teach: how the kingdom comes and how it grows; the good news of God's love for all his children, especially the poor and the despised; about the sacrifice and service required of those who would dwell in the kingdom; the need to be prepared for the coming kingdom; and about salvation and eternal life.

A parable, as we have noted, is based on a comparison. The very word *parable* is derived from the Greek *parabole*, "a putting beside," which itself is a translation of the Hebrew *mashal*, "to be similar." Allegories are also based on comparisons, but allegories and parables differ in that an allegory yields its meaning only through an interpretation of its details, while a parable conveys a single truth by means of its entire story. To the parable of the Sower (Mk 4:2-9) an allegorical interpretation of the four types of soil has been added (Mk 4:14-20), possibly by some later follower of Jesus. Be that as it may, here a true parable and a true allegory exist side by side.

For centuries, churchmen interpreted the parables allegorically, searching for a symbolic meaning in each detail, and thereby often missing the main thrust of the parable. Today, however, we search for the one message expressed by the story. We also try to interpret it in its historical setting. As Professor A.M. Hunter says in his book, *The Parables Then and Now*, "The true background of Jesus' parables is the great campaign of the kingdom of God, with Jesus as its spearhead, against the kingdom of evil."

Lists of parables vary in length from twenty-seven to as many as a hundred because some scholars include metaphors and similes in their lists. There are many of these striking expressions: "blind guides" and "whitewashed tombs" (Mt 23:24,27), "good measure pressed down, shaken together, running over" (Lk 6:38), "sift you like wheat" (Lk 22:31). Some of these may be relics of parables that were once fully developed stories.

In the lists below it will be noted that Matthew and Luke contain the most parables, while John, which is rich in striking metaphors, is credited with the fewest and these few are little more than fragments.

Parables Recorded in Three Gospels

	Matthew	Mark	Luke	John
Tasteless Salt	5:13	9:50	14:34-35	
The Lamp Under a Bushel	5:15-16	4:21-22	8:16-17	
The Patched Garment	9:16	2:21	5:36	
New Wine in Old Wineskins	9:17	2:22	5:37-38	
Plundering a Strong Man's House	12:29	3:27	11:21-22	
The Sower	13:3-23	4:2-20	8:4-15	
The Mustard Seed	13:31-32	4:30-32	13:18-19	
The Wicked Tenants of the Vineyard	21:33-45	12:1-12	20:9-19	
The Fig Tree as a Herald of Summer	24:32-33	13:28-29	21:29-31	

Parables Recorded in Two Gospels

	Matthew	Mark	Luke	John
Making Friends with Your Accuser	5:25-26		12:57-59	
The House Built on a Rock	7:24-27		6:47-49	
Children in the Market Place	11:16-17		7:31-32	
Leaven	13:33		13:20-21	
The Lost Sheep	18:12-14		15:3-7	
The Marriage Feast—Great Banquet	22:1-14		14:16-24	

	Matthew	Mark	Luke	John
The Thief at Night	24:43-44		12:39-40	
The Wise and Wicked Stewards	24:45-51		12:42-48	
Money Left in Trust	25:14-30		19:11-27	
The Waiting Servants		13:34-37	12:35-38	

Parables Recorded in One Gospel

	Matthew	Mark	Luke	John
Weeds among the Wheat	13:24-30			
Treasure Hidden in a Field	13:44			
The Pearl of Great Price	13:45-46			
The Dragnet	13:47-50			
The Unforgiving Servant	18:23-35			
The Laborers in the Vineyard	20:1-16			
The Father and Two Sons	21:28-32			
The Wise and Foolish Maidens	25:1-13			
The Seed Growing Secretly		4:26-29		
The Two Debtors			7:41-43	
The Good Samaritan			10:25-37	
The Friend at Midnight			11:5-10	
The Rich Fool			12:16-21	
The Watchful Servants			12:35-38	
The Barren Fig Tree			13:6-9	
On Building a Tower			14:28-30	
A King Goes to War			14:31-32	

Parables Recorded in One Gospel (continued)

	Matthew	Mark	Luke	John
The Lost Coin			15:8-10	
The Prodigal Son			15:11-32	
The Unjust Steward			16:1-13	
The Rich Man and Lazarus			16:19-31	
The Master and Servant			17:7-10	
The Unjust Judge			18:1-8	
The Pharisee and Tax Collector			18:9-14	
The Apprenticed Son				5:19-20
The Bread of Life				6:26-27
The True Shepherd				10:1-5
The Grain of Wheat				12:24
The Traveler Overtaken by Night				12:35
The Vine and Branches				15:1-6
The Woman in Labor				16:21

The Miracles of Jesus

How shall we regard the miracle stories of the Gospels? What do they mean? Did they really happen? It is impossible to ignore the thirty-five or more "mighty works" that the Gospels attribute to Jesus because these stories are not accidental, but form an integral part of the record. In the section above, entitled *Deeds and Words of Jesus Christ*, the "miracles" of the Lord are indicated by a star.

In our time, when a scientific understanding of the world dominates our thinking, stories of divine interventions that appear to be contrary to the laws of nature are dismissed by many people as the myths of a credulous, unsophisticated era. Most of us realize, however, that everything in the world is in some sense miraculous. Because we have witnessed many "miracles" of modern medicine, and turned the dials on our television sets to watch men walk on the moon, we no longer say "impossible" to something we cannot comprehend. Consequently, though we question everything, we approach the miracles with open minds.

The most helpful clue to an understanding of what the miracles really are is found in the answer Jesus made to messengers sent to him from John the Baptist. John had proclaimed the coming of One mightier than himself, the long-awaited Messiah. However, the news that reached John while he languished in a dungeon as a prisoner of Herod Antipas made him question if Jesus were indeed the fiery, conquering Messiah he had foretold. His messengers asked Jesus, "Are you he who is to come, or shall we look for another?" (Mt 11:3).

Characteristically, Jesus answered neither yes nor no, but challenged the men to draw their own conclusions, saying,

"Go tell John what you hear and see." Then, in words quoted in part from Isaiah's celebration of the coming of the Lord (Is 35:5-6), Jesus pointed to his own deeds, "The blind receive their sight and the lame walk, lepers are cleansed and the deaf hear, and the dead are raised up, and the poor have the good news preached to them" (Mt 11:4-5).

This reply of Jesus not only links his mission to Israel's ancient hope that God will clearly reveal himself to his people, but it summarizes both aspects of his mission: his preaching of the Good News and his acts demonstrating the meaning of that News. The words explain the deeds; the deeds illustrate and authenticate the words. "Accept the evidence of my deeds," he urged, "even if you do not believe me" (Jn 10:38, NEB). He taught that the reign of God had already begun and that proofs of its presence were already visible. The deeds he performed, the miracles, manifested the new order of life he brought to humanity.

The kingdom of God involves the health of people's minds and bodies as well as their souls. It is not only for the strong, the young, and the healthy; it welcomes also those who are weak, crippled, poor, and hopeless. There was boundless compassion in his acts, yet he did not go about merely doing good. When he freed the mentally afflicted from what people then believed to be possession by a devil, it was not just a single victory over the powers of evil that the cure signified. The wonderful things he did gave concrete evidence of wholeness of body and mind—of salvation. As Hans Küng the theologian states, "The kingdom of God is creation healed." The miracles showed what the kingdom would be like. In themselves they are the kingdom of God in action.

Jesus was far different from the popular miracle-workers of his time. He tried in vain to keep the news of his cures from being spread abroad (Mk 1:40-45). In his temptation

The Miracles of Jesus 131

he refused to turn stones into bread to satisfy his own hunger in the desert. He also rejected the suggestion that he hurl himself from a pinnacle of the Temple to prove his divine power (Mt 4:1-11), for it was never his way to compel faith in himself. When the scribes and Pharisees demanded of him a "sign" that he was the Messiah he refused (Mk 8:11-12). Marvels alone do not produce true faith. Finally, on the cross he endured the bystanders' taunt, "If you are the Son of God, come down from the cross" (Mt 27:40). Had he done all that people demanded or expected of him there would have been no Good News of the reign of God.

What actually happened in each miracle story is now probably impossible to discover. Undoubtedly there is a core of actual fact in each, a fact that the evangelists and others very likely elaborated and heightened, partly to satisfy the deep human craving for magic and the marvellous, but also to celebrate and magnify the power and glory of Christ. In any case, his early followers were not concerned primarily with medical details, nor did they offer explanations. It did not disturb them that sometimes the laws of nature seemed to be set aside. They expected that. What kind of fever did Peter's mother-in-law have? And by what methods was she healed? Was Jairus' little daughter actually dead or, as Jesus himself said, "not dead but sleeping" (Lk 8:52)? Though these are questions we cannot answer, we can discover from the Gospels the circumstances in which the miracles were performed.

These wonderful works took place in an atmosphere of heightened excitement and expectation that apparently surrounded Jesus. People responded to his extraordinary personality. They had faith in him. This was not true in Nazareth, for we read, "He could do no mighty work there, except that he laid his hands upon a few sick people and healed them. And he marveled because of their unbelief" (Mk 6:5-6). Elsewhere, however, we note that in the presence of Jesus, his disciples and the bystanders were "amazed" and "filled with awe," even "dumbfounded" and "awestruck," for they felt in him the reality of God's power.

In the Gospel of John, the miracles seem to be presented in a spiritual dimension, virtually as sacramental acts that convey eternal truth. William Temple, a recent Archbishop of Canterbury, in his *Readings in St. John's Gospel* writes of the miracles, "'Sign' is the word chosen by St. John to describe them, and he thus warns us that their meaning is something beyond themselves. Moreover the fact that he selects seven is a way of telling his readers that they are not to be read as mere episodes but as conveying a special truth which finds expression only in the whole series taken together."

These seven "signs" show us God's power working through Jesus to heal, to sustain, and to enrich human life. His presence at the wedding feast in Cana (Jn 2:1-11) brought added joy, for he indeed turns the ordinary "water" of life into "wine." Faith in him is necessary for wholeness and healing, faith like that of the military official whose son Jesus healed (Jn 4:46-54). He restores those who are crippled in body or spirit, as he renewed the lost powers of the man lying on a pallet beside the Pool of Bethzatha (Jn 5:2-9). To those who hunger for the bread of life he offers abundant food, as he fed a multitude of five thousand people beyond the Sea of Galilee (Jn 6:1-14). He is Lord even of the elements and to those who need him, he brings the help of his presence, as once, walking on the water, he came to his frightened disciples (Jn 6:15-21). He gives sight to the spiritually blind, as he healed the man born blind (Jn 9:1-7). The seventh "sign," the restoration of Lazarus to life, portrays Jesus as the giver of life and foreshadows that which towers above all miracles—his resurrection.

The Prayers of Jesus and His Followers

The prayers of the New Testament arise from the centuries-long prayer life of Israel. Jesus himself was nurtured in this rich tradition. The people into whose midst he was born were, according to the stories in Matthew and Luke, praying, worshiping people. They include Mary and Joseph, Zechariah and Elizabeth, devout Simeon, the prophetess Anna, those who looked for redemption, and finally, the Wise Men. These travelers of another faith must have been men of prayer, for at the heart of all religion there is prayer. Surely, in his home and at the synagogue school in Nazareth Jesus was taught the psalms. In the Sabbath services of the town synagogue—the focal point of Jewish spiritual life—he undoubtedly joined in the prayers and thanksgivings of the elders.

When he became a man, his close relationship to God seems to have been such that prayer for him was continuous. Even so, the Gospels record that he joined regularly in the Sabbath worship of the synagogue (Lk 4:16). Frequently, he left the distractions and pressures of his ministry to go apart to pray in peace and solitude (Mk 1:35; Mt 14:23; Lk 5:16). Luke's Gospel notes specifically that Jesus prayed at important moments in his life: at his baptism (3:21), before calling his disciples (6:12), before many of his miracles (9:18), at his transfiguration (9:28), during the last supper (22:19), in Gethsemane (22:40-46), and at his crucifixion (23:34,46).

One day, his disciples, having observed him in prayer, came to him and asked, "Lord, teach us to pray, as John taught his disciples" (Lk 11:1).

"Pray like this," he said and gave them that most compact and, at the same time, most comprehensive of prayers we now call the Lord's Prayer (Mt 6:9-13; Lk 11:2-4). This familiar series of petitions is similar in form to the synagogue litanies, yet is filled with Jesus' unique message. It is a model prayer, the perfect pattern of Christian supplication, and the basic type for longer and more detailed prayers. Jesus indicated that first we should realize the presence of God our Father, living, loving, already present, and seeking us out. The Lord's Prayer reaches a climax in the petitions: "Thy kingdom come. Thy will be done, on earth as it is in heaven." In this earnest assent to the will of God we not only hear an echo of Mary's prayer, "Let it be to me according to your word" (Lk 1:38), but we are reminded of the prayer of Jesus in Gethsemane, "Father, if thou art willing, remove this cup from me; nevertheless not my will, but thine, be done" (Lk 22:42).

The Gospels record that Jesus taught by precept and parable that prayer should be: earnest, persevering, humble, private, simple, sincere, and offered in faith and with a forgiving spirit (Lk 11:5-13; 18:1,9-14; Mt 6:5-8; Mk 11:24-26). He assured people that when "two or three are gathered in my name there am I in the midst of them" (Mt 18:19-20). He promised that prayer offered in his name (meaning, in accordance with his spirit) and the prayers of those who abide in him will be answered (Jn 14:13; 15:7).

The early Church was alive with prayer that transformed the followers of Christ and endowed them with the wisdom and strength to launch the Christian movement (Acts 1:14,24; 4:31 etc.) Praying and prayer are specifically mentioned some eighty times in Acts and the Letters. Paul usually begins his letters with a prayerful salutation and ends them with a prayerlike blessing. In Romans, Paul explains to those who find prayer difficult that the indwelling Spirit interprets a person's uncertain, inarticulate, and deepest longings and "intercedes for us . . . according to the will of God" (Rom 8:26-27).

The Bible ends with what must be one of the Church's oldest petitions, a prayer for Christ's coming, "Come, Lord Jesus!" (Rev 22:20).

From first to last the Bible demonstrates that religion involves a reaching out toward some transcendent and powerful Being—toward God—in an attempt to enter into spiritual communion with him and bring before him our world and our own personal needs and desires as well as those of other people. The Bible suggests that prayer opens human lives to an inflow of God's grace. Prayer is sometimes silent, wordless, contemplative. Often it is a natural outpouring of religious feeling in words. Whatever the quality of prayer or whatever form it takes, it involves passionate, compassionate, responsible thought. This is the kind of thought that frees us from bondage to ourselves and the trivialities of our days. Prayer lifts us up to perceive the wholeness of life and causes us to perceive the reality of God.

New Testament Prayers

Mary - acceptance of God's will	Lk 1:38
Simeon - recognition of Christ	Lk 2:29-32
The Lord's Prayer	Mt 6:9-13; Lk 11:2-4
Jesus - thanksgiving	Mt 11:25-26; Lk 10:21
The Pharisee - self-congratulation	Lk 18:11
The Tax Collector - for mercy	Lk 18:13
Jesus - thanksgiving for God's acceptance of unspoken prayer	Jn 11:41
- that God's name be glorified	Jn 12:27-28
- "Father, the hour has come . . ."	Jn 17
- "not my will, but thine, be done"	Mt 26:39,42; Mk 14:36; Lk 22:42
- for those who crucified him	Lk 23:34
- cry of abandonment	Mt 27:46; Mk 15:34
- prayer of commitment	Lk 23:46
The Apostles - for divine guidance	Acts 1:24-25
The Church - for courage to speak God's word	Acts 4:24-30
Stephen - prayers before death	Acts 7:59,60
Paul - at his conversion	Acts 22:8,10
Ananias - for assurance	Acts 9:10,13-14
Paul - for the Christians in Rome	Rom 15:5-6,13,33
- benediction	Rom 16:25-27
- for the Lord's coming	1 Cor 16:21
- thanksgivings	2 Cor 2:14; 9:15
- for peace in the Church	Gal 6:16

- for spiritual wisdom and vision — Eph 1:16-23
- for strengthening through the Spirit — Eph 3:14-21
- for spiritual gifts — Phil 1:9-11
- for insight into the will of God — Col 1:9-12
- for an opening to preach — Col 4:3-4
Epaphros - for spiritual maturity — Col 4:12
Paul - for the Thessalonians — 1 Thess 3:10-13; 5:23; 2 Thess 1:11-12; 2:16-17; 3:5

Blessing of the faithful — Heb 13:20-21
Encouragement for those facing suffering — 1 Pet 5:10-11
John - for total well-being — 3 Jn v.2
Jude - benediction and doxology — Jude vv. 24-25
John - for the coming of Christ — Rev 22:20

An Outline of the Life of Paul

The primary source for our knowledge of Paul consists of his nine genuine letters: Romans, 1 and 2 Corinthians, Galatians, Philippians, Colossians, 1 and 2 Thessalonians, and Philemon. There is little historical information in Ephesians, which may or may not be by Paul. The Pastoral Letters, 1 and 2 Timothy and Titus, though probably written by one of Paul's disciples, undoubtedly contain actual fragments from Paul's correspondence.

The secondary source for the facts of Paul's life is the Acts of the Apostles with its detailed accounts of the great apostle's conversion and his far-flung missionary labors. When we fit the two sources together we discover not only fairly long periods of time for which there is no information, but also some minor inconsistencies. These latter include such matters as his movements after his conversion and the number of his visits to Jerusalem. Acts mentions five visits, Galations only two. In 2 Cor 11:23-28, Paul refers to his hardships and sufferings, very few of which are mentioned in Acts. The Pastoral Letters, moreover, include fragments from Paul that are difficult to fit into an outline of his life (2 Tim 1:15-18; 4:6-21; Titus 1:5; 3:12-13). Nevertheless, the facts provided by the primary and secondary sources give us a fuller account of his life than that of any other early follower of Christ.

Belonging as Paul did to three cultures—Jewish, Greek, and Roman—he was uniquely qualified to understand the message of Christ, to interpret it to Greek-speaking people, and to carry the good news to the far reaches of the Roman world. Saul—to call him by his Hebrew name—was fiercely proud of his Jewish origin. He was born and brought up in the Hellenistic city of Tarsus, the cosmopolitan capital of

An Outline of the Life of Paul

Cilicia where the teeming life of the East met the classical culture of Greece. Legally, Paul or Paulus (his Roman surname) was a Roman, having inherited this prized citizenship from his father, who probably received it for some outstanding service to the state. During Paul's career, his Roman citizenship became virtually a passport giving him a safer and freer access to the Gentile world he tried to win for Christ than many other Christians enjoyed (Acts 22:24-29).

1. Early Life
   a. Born of Jewish parents in Tarsus (c.A.D.10-15), Phil 3:5; Acts 22:3
   b. Taught trade of a tentmaker, Acts 18:3
   c. Educated as a rabbi in Jerusalem, Acts 22:3; 26:4-5
   d. Witnesses the stoning of Stephen, Acts 7:58-8:1; 22:20
   e. Persecutes the Church, Gal 1:13-14; 1 Tim 1:13; Acts 7:58-8:3; 9:1-2; 22:4-5; 26:9-12

2. His conversion (c.A.D.35), Gal 1:13-17; Acts 9:1-19; 22:5-16; 26:12-18

3. Period of preparation
   a. Withdraws to "Arabia," Gal 1:15-17
   b. Preaches in Damascus, 2 Cor 11:32-33; Acts 9:19-25
   c. Visits Peter in Jerusalem, Gal 1:18-20; Acts 9:26-30
   d. Preaches in Syria and Cilicia, Gal 1:21-24

4. His mission in Antioch of Syria, Acts 11:21-30; 12:25-13:3

5. His second visit to Jerusalem (possibly Gal 2:1-10); Acts 11:30

6. The first missionary journey (c.A.D.47-49), Gal 4:13-14; 2 Tim 3:10-11; Acts 13:1-14:28

a. Itinerary: Island of Cyprus from Salamis to Paphos; Asia Minor: Perga, Antioch in Pisidia, Iconium, Lystra, Derbe; and return via Lystra, Iconium, Antioch, Perga, Attalia, to Antioch in Syria
   b. Companions: Barnabas, John Mark
 7. His third visit to Jerusalem for the Church Council, Gal 2:1-10; Acts 15:1-35
 8. The second missionary journey (c.A.D.50-52), Acts 15:36-18:22; 1 Thess 2:17-3:3
   a. Itinerary: through Syria and Cilicia; to Derbe, Lystra; through Phrygia and probably North Galatia in Central Asia Minor to Troas; past Samothrace to Neapolis; Philippi, Thessalonica, Beroea, Athens, a year and a half in Corinth; Ephesus, Caesarea.
   b. Letters written during this period; 1 and 2 Thessalonians, Galatians
   c. Companions: Silas, Timothy, Luke (?)
 9. His fourth visit to Jerusalem and brief stay in Antioch, Acts 18:22
10. The third missionary journey (c.A.D.53-58), 2 Cor 1:8-10; Acts 18:23-21:16
   a. Itinerary: the churches in Galatia and Phrygia, two years in Ephesus, Macedonia, Corinth (1 Cor 16:6; or 2 Cor 2:1; 12:14), possibly Illyricum (modern Yugoslavia) (Rom 15:19), Philippi, Troas, Assos, Mitylene, Samos, Miletus, Cos, Rhodes, Patara, Tyre, Ptolemais, Caesarea, Jerusalem
   b. Letters written: 1 and 2 Corinthians (from Ephesus), Romans (from Corinth), Philippians, Colossians, Philemon (from prison in Ephesus or later from Caesarea or Rome)
11. His fifth visit to Jerusalem (c.A.D.58), Rom 15:25; Acts 20:22-23; 21:8-23:35

a. The riot and his arrest
   b. His speeches to the mob and before the Sanhedrin
   c. His transfer to Caesarea after his nephew's warning
12. Imprisonment in Caesarea (c.A.D.58-60), Acts 23:33-26:32
   a. His hearing before Felix the governor
   b. His appeal to Caesar in the second hearing
   c. His defense before Agrippa and Bernice
13. Paul's voyage to Rome (c.A.D.60-61), Acts 27-28
   a. Companions: Luke (?), Aristarchus, and the centurion guard Julius
   b. Route: Caesarea, Sidon, past Cyprus, Myra in Lycia, past island of Cnidus to Fair Havens on Crete, past Cauda, storm in Mediterranean, shipwreck on Malta, Syracuse, Rhegium, Puteoli, the Forum of Appius, Three Taverns, Rome
   c. Paul's last letter from Rome (?), 2 Tim 4:6-18
14. A possible unrecorded journey to Spain, Rom 15:24-29
15. Paul's imprisonment and martyrdom in Rome (c.A.D. 64), according to various Church traditions.

Selected Bibliography

The Bible dictionaries, concordances, atlases, and commentaries suggested in *Introducing the Bible*, which is Volume I of this series, together with many other reference books of a similar nature, offer invaluable information to Bible readers. For further light on the New Testament, the following books are suggested.

Coggan, Donald F., *The Prayers of the New Testament*. New York: Harper and Row, 1975.

Davis, W. D., *Invitation to the New Testament: A Guide to its Main Witnesses.* New York: Doubleday and Co., Inc., Anchor Books, 1969.

Dodd, Charles H., *The Apostolic Preaching and Its Developments.* New York: Harper and Row, 1960.

--- *The Parables of the Kingdom.* New York: Charles Scribner's Sons, The Scribner Library, 1961.

Hunter, Archibald M., *Introducing the New Testament.* Philadelphia, Westminster Press, 1957.

--- *The Parables Then and Now.* London: SCM Press, Ltd., 1971.

Kee, Howard Clark; Young, Franklin W.; Froehlich, Karlfried, *Understanding the New Testament.* 3rd ed. Englewood Cliffs, New Jersey: Prentice-Hall, 1973.

Mann, C. S., *The Man for All Time.* Wilton, CT: Morehouse-Barlow Co., Inc., 1971

_____ , *The Message Delivered.* Wilton, CT: Morehouse-Barlow Co., Inc., 1973

Richardson, Alan., *The Miracle Stories of the Gospels.* New York: Harper and Row, 1942.

Taylor, Vincent., *The Life and Ministry of Jesus.* Nashville: Abingdon Press, 1955.

Throckmorton, Burton H.; Cadbury, Henry J.; Grant, Frederick C.; and Craig, Clarence T., *Gospel Parallels: A Synopsis of the First Three Gospels.* New York: Thomas Nelson and Sons, 1957.

Index

Acts, Book of, 12, 13, 41-47, 138
Allegories vs. parables, 124-25
Antioch, Chalice of, 28; of Syria, 16, 24
Anti-Semitism, 21
Apocalypse, of John, 105-10; in Matthew, 21; of Paul, 77
Apostles' Creed, 95-96
Apostolic message, 12, 59
Aramaic, 19, 26
Athens, 44, 74
Augustine, Saint, 52
Authorship, fictitious, 81, 98

Barnabas, 24

Caesarea, 46
Carrington, Philip, 108
"Catholic Epistles," 14; *see also* James, 1 and 2 Peter, 1, 2, 3, John, Jude
Chalice of Antioch, 27-28
Christ, see Jesus Christ
Christian faith, statement of, 68
Christian freedom, Magna Charta of, 53
Christianity vs. Judaism, 61-62, 88-89
Christian life, living the, 72, 81-82, 92-93
Chronology, in John, 37-38; in Mark, 25, 112
Church, the, 21; concept of, 65; expansion of, in Acts, 43; in Matthew, 21; the ministry of, 86; organization of, 80; universality of, 21
Clement of Alexandria, 37
Coggan, Donald, 108
Colossians, Letter to the, 64, 70-73, 138
Corinth, 49, 53-54, 74-75
Corinthians, 1st Letter to the 52-56, 138
Corinthians, 2nd Letter to the, 56-59, 138
Courtyard of Fortress Antonia, 40
Creche, 32, 34

Daniel, 107
Dante, 31, 108
Deeds and Words of Jesus Christ, 112-21
Discourses, in John, figurative, 38; in Matthew, 17-18
Dodd, Charles H., 18, 49, 64
Domitian, emperor, 95, 107, 108 Doxology, 105

Ecumenical movement, 65
Elder, the, 101, 102, 103
Ephesians, Letter to the, 63-66, 138
Ephesus, 39, 44, 51, 64, 67, 100
Epistles, *see* Letters
Erasmus, 55
Ezekiel, 107

Faith, essentials of, in Romans, 49; of Gospel writers, 13; in Hebrews, 90; vs. works, 92-93

Famine relief, 47, 50
Forged letter, 78
Francis, Saint, 32, 34
Four Horsemen of Apocalypse, 109

Galatians, Letter to the, 60-62, 138
Gentile Christians, 21, 26, 61, 64
Gnosticism, 71, 100, 104-5
God, Son of, 13, 26
Good news, 11, 12, 13, 130
Gospel, derivation of, 12
Gospels, harmony of, 112-21; purpose of, 13
Greek language, 12, 19, 31, 93

Harmony of the Gospels, 112-21
Hebrews, Letter to the, 14, 87-91
Henry VIII, 91
Heresy, 71-72, 92, 100, 104-5
Herod Antipas, 129
Herod the Great, 40
Historical value, of Acts, 46-47; of Mark, 25
Holy Grail, 27
Holy Spirit, 43, 80
Hospitality, 84-85
Humanitarian emphasis, 31-32
Humankind, oneness of, 110
Hunter, A.M., 125
Hutchinson, Anne, 56

Immortality, Paul's statement on, 55

James, Letter of, 91-93
Jerusalem, 38
Jesse, 34
Jesus Christ, deeds and words of, 11, 18, 24, 112-21; message of, 11; miracles of, 11, 129-32; parables of, 122-28; portrait of, 13, 18-19, 26, 38, 123; prayers of, 133-37; proclamation of the kingdom by, 11, 12, 26; resurrection of, 55; sayings of, 18, 19, 26; teachings of, 12, 18-19
John, the apostle, 35, 100, 107
John, author of Revelation, 107
John, the Baptist, 129
John, the Divine, 107
John, the Elder of Ephesus, 25, 39, 100
John, the evangelist, 39
John, Gospel of, 12, 35-41
John, 1st Letter of, 14, 99-101
John, 2nd Letter of, 14, 101-2
John, 3rd Letter of, 14, 102-3
John Mark, 24
Joseph of Arimathea, 27
Judaism vs. Christianity, 32, 61-62, 88-89
Judas, brother of James of Jerusalem, 105

143

Jude, Letter of, 14, 103-5
Justification by faith, 62, 92, 93

Keller, Helen, 101
Kingdom of God, as key to the parables, 124; miracles and the, 130; proclamation of the, 11, 12, 26; worldwide, 21
Küng, Hans, 130

Last supper, 38, 55
Latimer, Hugh, 91
Law of Old Testament, 18, 19, 61
Letters, "Catholic," 14, 91-105; encyclical, 64; vs. Epistles, 13; forged, 78; Pastoral, 13, 79-85, 138; Paul's, 12, 13, 48-87, 138
Life in the 1st century, in Acts, 44
Lincoln, Abraham, 47
Logia, 18, 19
Lord's Prayer, 134
Love, Paul's hymn on, 55, 56; in 1 John, 101
Luke, Gospel of, 12, 18, 24, 28-34
Luke, Paul's companion, 30
Luther, Martin, 62, 93, 94

Magna Charta, Galatians as Christian, 62
Mark, Gospel of, 12, 17, 22-28, 30, 112
Mark, John, 24-25
Marriage, Christian, 21, 66
Mary Queen of Scots, 96
Matthew, Gospel of, 12, 16-22, 24
Message of Jesus, 11
Messiah, 19, 129
Milton, 108
Miracles of Jesus, 11, 129-32; as kingdom of God in action, 130; clue to understanding of, 129; in Gospel of John, 132; list of, 112-21

Nero, 95, 98
New Testament, books of, 12-14; prayers of 136-37; theme of, 11-12

Onesimus, 71, 86
Origen, 89
Ossuary in British Museum, 40

Palestine, life in, as recorded in the parables, 123-24
Papias, Bishop, 18, 19, 25, 39
Parables, 122-28
Pastoral Letters, 13, 79-82, 138
Paul, 12, 13, 24, 30, 39, 43, 44, 46; apostleship of, 58-59; as known by contemporaries, 59; letters of, 12, 48-87, 138; life of, an outline of, 138-41; personal faith of, 69; prison letters of, 72; spiritual insights of, 62
Peter, 24, 25, 26, 27, 43, 44, 95
Peter, 1st Letter of, 14, 24, 93-96
Peter, 2nd Letter of, 14, 96-98
Persecution, 95, 107
Petrels, 22
Philadelphia, 109

Philemon, Letter to, 64, 85-87, 138
Philippi of Macedonia, 43, 68
Philippians, Letter to the, 66-69, 138
Phoebe, 51
Portico of Temple, 40
Prayer in Luke, 32
Prayers of Jesus and his followers, 133-37
Prison letters of Paul. *See* Philippians, Colossians, Philemon, Ephesians

Q Source of Gospels, 18, 19, 30

Resurrection, oldest record of, 55
Revelation, Book of, 14, 105-10
Roman army of occupation, 21
Roman church, 50
Romans, Letter to the, 48-52, 138
Rome, 24, 43, 46, 49, 64, 67, 95
Roosevelt, Franklin D., 56

Sanhedrin, 21
Sayings of Jesus, 18, 19
Scott, Ernest F., 81
Second coming of Christ, 75, 77, 84, 97
Sequence of events in Mark, 25, 112
Sermon on the Mount, 16, 92
"Signs" in John, 38, 132
Simony, 47
Silas, 43, 74, 95
Silvanus, *see* Silas
Slavery, 86-87
Son of God, 13, 26
Speeches in Acts, 46
Synopsis of Gospels, 112-21
Synoptic Gospels, 37, 38; *see also* Matthew, Mark, Luke

Teachings of Jesus, 12; 18-19
Temple, William, 132
Tennyson, 123
Tentmaking, 76
Theme of New Testament, 11
Theophilus, 30, 42
Thessalonians, 1st Letter to the, 73-76, 138
Thessalonians, 2nd Letter to the, 76-78, 138
Timothy, companion of Paul, 74-75
Timothy, 1st Letter to, 13, 79-82, 138
Timothy, 2nd Letter to, 13, 80-83, 138
Titus, Letter to, 13, 80-82, 84-85, 138
Traditions, early Christian, 19, 37
Trinity, 90
Twelve, the, 105
Tychicus, 64, 71, 86

Universal message of Church, 21, 31, 44

Visions, 107
von Hügel, Friedrich, 68

"We" passages of Acts, 30, 46
Women, role of, in Church, 32, 51, 68, 69, 80
Wonderful works of Jesus, 11, 112-21, 129-32